FLY HIGH FIREFLY

KYRA FAITH

FLY HIGH FIREFLY

To my lovely family and friends who have always supported me.
To every child who battles chronic medical conditions and to their families and the nurses that care for them. They are the true superheroes.

Copyright © 2025 by Kyra Faith
All rights reserved. No part of this book may be reproduced in any manner whatsoever without written permission except in the case of brief quotations embodied in critical articles and reviews.
First Printing, 2025

PROLOGUE: FOREVER FIREFLY

A black pool of hundreds of brilliant, little lights hung over us and all around us. Nights in North Carolina—with the twinkling stars and the glowing fireflies—are truly heavenly. With the lanterns turned off, nothing around me was perceptible. But the warmth of my daughter nestled in the crook of my arm and the sound of her calm, even breaths gave me comfort. I wrapped my arms around her and squeezed her pudgy toddler arms.

I smiled as images of her chasing fireflies just moments before replayed in my mind. Upon catching one, her eyes would grow wide, and she would watch in awe at the silent, pulsating glow before releasing it back into the sky and whispering, "Fly high, firefly!". By saying that, she believed she was sending the fireflies up to heaven. It was her absolute favorite thing to do.

"I love you, Ari," I whispered into the darkness.

"I love you, too, Muma," she sweetly whispered back.

She turned to snuggle into my underarm, briefly giggling. "I love watching the sky with you!"

"Me too, honey. Me too."

"It's our forever thing. Promise?"

"That's right, sweetie. I promise. Stargazing always and forever, you and I."

I kissed the top of her head—her soft, voluminous curls brushing against my lips. My heart was full. I looked to the heavenly sky above and smiled.

* * *

A familiar hand gently shook my shoulder, and a flashlight shined brightly over my face. I squinted and covered my eyes with my free hand.

"Hey, Norah," my husband spoke softly, kneeling down. "I just wanted to check on you. It's late. Looks like you and Arielle both fell asleep while stargazing. I just put Emilia to bed; she fell asleep during our movie. Why don't you head inside, honey. I'll carry Ari to bed."

"Ok. Thanks, Ivaan." I leaned forward to kiss his forehead and then breathed in deeply, yawning.

As Ivaan bent down, I felt the warm weight on my arm leave me. His footsteps grew distant. My arm was tight with pain as I brought it out of its outstretched position and draped it across my stomach. I sat up and rolled over onto my knees just in time to see the beam of the flashlight disappear into the house. Realizing I was alone, I quickly grabbed the blanket and lantern and headed inside.

I entered my and Ivaan's room and sleepily undressed, slipping on my lavender-purple nightgown. I lazily brushed my teeth and climbed into our soft, inviting bed. Just as I laid down on my back, Ivaan walked in with a T-shirt and navy blue plaid pajama pants on. Even in his pajamas, he managed to look charming. My heart beat faster.

"Hello, handsome," I whispered.

"Hello, beautiful," he replied.

"Are the girls asleep?"

"Yep, far away in Dreamland being princesses, I'm sure." He grinned.

"Thanks, honey. What did I ever do to deserve you?"

He chuckled. "Oh, Nor, I'm more than sure that I should be asking you that question." He climbed into bed and leaned down, smoothing back my hair before kissing me delicately. His lips were smooth, his breath minty. Slowly, he lifted away and stared lovingly into my eyes. His vibrant green eyes and sharply-shaped face made me feel alive. My heart beat faster. He smiled dashingly and turned to lay down beside me.

"Goodnight, sweetheart."

"Goodnight, my love." I turned off the bedside lamp and rolled over onto my side, laying my hand on his chest and my head on his shoulder. The rhythm of his breathing became my sole focus: in and out, in and out.

God has been so good to me I thought as sleep claimed all of my senses.

PART 1: FLY AND FALL

10 days later...

UNUSUAL THINGS

I watched as the girls raced up our driveway, their Sunday dresses fluttering eloquently in the morning breeze. Emilia reached the front door first with the help of her tall and lanky legs. She threw her arms in the air, jumping up and down and giggling. Arielle mounted the steps to the porch and immediately fell to her knees panting.

I let go of Ivaan's hand and quickened my pace.

"Ari, honey, did you fall? Are you alright?" Concern creased my forehead.

"No, Muma, I didn't fall. My legs are just tired." She was still panting and her face was pale.

"Ok, honey. Let's go inside and get some water. Then we'll get changed and go out for brunch. I think you just need some fuel; you didn't eat much last night."

Still panting, she gave a slow nod as Ivaan scooped her up into his muscular arms, touched my shoulder reassuringly, and carried her inside.

Unphased, Emilia looked up at me. "Mum, can we go to the playground after we eat?"

"Sure, honey, that sounds lovely. Just promise me you'll at least eat some of your vegetables this time."

Her smile faded momentarily as she pondered this trade off. "Ok, fine. But please don't make me eat the green trees," she pleaded.

"Ok, no broccoli," I laughed. "I suppose I can work with that. Now go get changed, Em, before I get so hungry I have to eat you!" I said as I raised my arms and took slow, straddled steps towards her.

"Ahhhh! Mummy monster!" She screamed and ran into the house giggling, her thin pigtails bouncing as she skipped up the stairs.

I shook my head, smiling.

Then reality hit me, and I thought of Arielle's unusual tiredness, paleness, stomach aches, and lack of appetite over the last couple of days. I took a strained breath, and I prayed to God that my baby was ok.

* * *

The slashing of the teppanyaki chef's tools upon the hot cooking surface thrilled everyone at the table. He tossed a spatula up in the air, caught it, and started to effortlessly slice carrots, onion, and zucchini. Everyone clapped.

To amuse the children, he stacked a tower of the rings of onion and poured in some water, which made smoke spew out of the top like a volcano. The kids' eyes widened.

Then he poured soy sauce into the heap of vegetables and mixed in some broccoli.

"Eww, veggies," Emilia complained, crinkling her nose.

"Remember our deal," I winked.

She crossed her arms on the table and rested her chin on her arms in defeat. But then her eyes widened.

"Ari! Do you want to play an obstacle course game when we go to the playground after we eat?" She raised her eyebrows expectantly.

"Yeah!" Ari exclaimed, then quickly grew serious. "But, Em, don't make it so hard like last time."

"Ok, ok. But make mine hard since I'm seven. Because three year olds get the easy level and seven year olds get the hard level."

Ari nodded in agreement. I looked at her pale face and her tired eyes. Then I noticed her arms crossed over her abdomen, and my heart ached. *What was going on with my sweet girl?*

The chef plating our food snapped me out of my thought spiral.

"Yum! This looks delicious!" Ivaan said with excitement as the chef piled vegetables, noodles, fried rice, and chicken onto his plate. "Let's dig in, girls!"

I ate quickly, though politely, and did not leave anything but a grain of rice on my plate. Ivaan had finished quickly, too, and Emilia was mostly finished but was still carefully fishing out every piece of broccoli from her small pile of vegetables.

I turned my gaze over to Arielle. Her plate was identical to when I had checked ten minutes ago: she had only eaten half of her noodles and a couple pieces of chicken. She had a blank stare on her face and still had her arms wrapped around her abdomen.

I breathed in deeply and locked eyes with Ivaan. He had sensed my distress. I knew he was worried too.

"Ari, sweetie, what's wrong? You love hibachi," Ivaan tried.

Ari slowly turned her head to look at Ivaan, then looked down at her plate.

"My tummy hurts, and I don't feel good." She frowned and looked up at us with puppy eyes. Tears streamed down her face when she blinked.

"Oh, honey," Ivaan replied, "I'm sorry you don't feel like yourself. We'll get you feeling better, though, don't worry."

I took hold of Ari in my arms and hugged her. "Don't cry, sweetie. How about you and I go home and watch a movie while Em and Daddy go to the park. I think you need to get some rest, honey."

She cried harder. "But I love playing at the park!"

"I know, honey, but I think you would feel better if you took it easy for the rest of the day."

She looked up at me, her cheeks wet with tears, and nodded.

* * *

I walked over to the couch where Arielle lay. She held her stuffed unicorn close against her belly, and she loosely gripped the corner of her purple blanket with her small hand. She had been sleeping on the couch ever since I took her back to the house after brunch.

Her cheeks were flushed. I lightly placed my hand on her forehead. She was warm.

I went to the bathroom upstairs and rummaged through the drawers, searching for the thermometer. I finally spotted it under a package of baby wipes and grabbed hold of it. I headed down the stairs quickly and scanned Arielle's forehead. My suspicion was confirmed: she had a fever. It was 101.4 degrees.

Oh, my poor baby. Her body must be trying to fight off a stubborn virus. Please, God, help her feel better soon.

CHAPTER 2

RUN ITS COURSE (4 DAYS LATER)

The receptionist handed me a clipboard of forms to fill out and told us to sit on the "SICK" side of the waiting room. I walked over to two cushioned chairs, gently set Arielle down, and plopped down in the chair next to her. Ari played a cat game on her pink iPad while I skimmed through the forms, updating information where needed. She hadn't seen her pediatrician since her three-year-old check-up and wasn't due for her four year one for another seven months. I checked the box that stated "Sick child visit", and I listed Ari's symptoms: fever, fatigue, loss of appetite, stomach pain. Then, I walked back up to the desk and gave the completed forms back to the receptionist.

"Thank you. It should only be a few minutes."

I nodded and went back to my seat, feeling Ari's forehead before sitting back down. She was warm, but not terribly so. I breathed out, slightly relieved.

"Muma, will it hurt?" she asked without looking up from her game.

"No, no, honey. No shots today. We just have to see what kind of germs are making you feel so yucky."

"That's good. I don't want to cry today."

"Aww, Ari, I don't want you to either," I said as I leaned down to kiss the top of her head.

The door swung open and a short, sturdy nurse with grey curly hair appeared. She squinted down at the clipboard in her hands. "Airy-elly," she called.

She hadn't pronounced Arielle's name correctly, but we were the only ones on the "SICK" side, so it had to be us.

"Come on, honey, I think that's us," I said, taking Ari by the hand.

The nurse grabbed her vitals, jotting down the numbers as she went. Once done, she shuffled down the hallway, leading us to an examination room. She entered Ari's vitals into the computer and then looked up, adjusting her thinly rimmed glasses.

"Alright," she said, "Dr. Henz should be with you guys in a few minutes."

She walked out, leaving the door cracked open behind her.

"Ok, honey, let me get you up on the table."

I grabbed her under her arms and lifted her up onto the examination table. The thin, white paper crinkled as I set her down.

She smiled as she pointed to the Disney princess decals on the wall. "Look, Muma!" she exclaimed.

"Wow, what a fitting room for my little princess!"

She giggled and put her arm up in a princess wave. Then she smiled, tilting her chin up.

I took on a playful English accent, "If you, my princess, prove to be brave during this next event, my royal guards will give you a prize!"

Her eyes widened, and she giggled. "I will be so brave, the whole kingdom will know!" she remarked in a pitchy voice, unable to mimic my English accent.

"Magnificent," I applauded, "I believe that you will."

I smiled, glad that she seemed to be perking up a bit.

Just then, there was a knock at the door and Dr. Henz entered. Her wavy black hair framed her dark, youthfully smooth skin, and her dark blue, thick-rimmed glasses held her kind brown eyes. Her red, heart-shaped lips curved up into a smile and then she spoke, "Hello, my most favorite family!" she exclaimed.

Dr. Henz had been my doctor and helped deliver both of my girls before she decided to switch over to pediatrics, so she has watched Arielle and Emilia grow up over the years. The girls love her, and so do I. She is young for a doctor but is so intelligent that she was able to graduate med school early at the top of her class. She is quite a lovely human being, and I have always felt comforted with my daughters being under her care.

"I see you haven't been feeling too great lately, huh?"

Ari shook her head, frowning.

"Aww, I don't like to hear that," Dr. Henz replied. "But don't worry, I'm sure we can get you back to your old self real soon." Then she turned to me. "So, Mama, what all has been going on with Ari that told you to bring her in?"

I took a deep breath in, "Well, I noticed a major shift in her energy levels a little over a week ago. She's been taking longer naps and tires quickly when playing. And she doesn't seem to have much of an appetite, so it's been hard to get her to eat very much at all. She also keeps complaining that her stomach hurts and that she just doesn't feel good. And she's started having fevers too." I paused, taking a breath. "All of this just has me worried because she's rarely ever sick, and it has been a week of these symptoms with no relief."

"I see, uh-huh," she said as she finished typing up some notes. "I'll tell you what, Mama, I'll listen to her lungs and everything, and I'll order a rapid test to check for the flu and swab her to check for strep. But since she isn't having any cold-like symptoms or a sore throat, I doubt those will come back positive. Since she has a fever, though, I just want to make sure we're not dealing with an atypical presentation. How does that sound?"

"That sounds great. Thank you so much, Dr. Henz."

"My pleasure. We've got to get sweet Ari feeling better, right?" she said and lightly touched Ari's knee.

Ari nodded and half-smiled.

Dr. Henz carefully conducted the examination, closing her eyes as she listened to Arielle's lungs and heart. Once done, she peeled off her blue gloves and threw them in the trash can.

"Her lungs and heart sound normal, and her ears, eyes, and throat look good too. So that is reassuring. I will have my nurse come in and do the swabs, and then I'll come back with the results and discuss next steps. Cool?" she asked with two thumbs up.

I nodded, and Ari gave two thumbs up back. Dr. Henz smiled and headed out, closing the door behind her.

* * *

Arielle was lying on the examination table on her back with her arms crossed behind her head and her knees bent with her feet flat on the table. Her iPad was propped up against her thighs; she was happily and intently watching Bluey.

There was a knock at the door and Dr. Henz walked in. Ari barely noticed. Dr. Henz sat in her desk chair and rolled next to me to deliver the results.

"As I suspected," she started, "both tests came back negative. That being the case, I believe that Arielle is dealing with gastroenteritis—commonly known as the stomach flu—which is a virus and can't really be treated with antibiotics. So, unfortunately, I think we will just have to let the virus run its course. But you can continue giving Tylenol for the fever when needed. I also see that her weight has dropped a little bit, but that is probably due to the shift in appetite. So I advise you to encourage Ari to eat when she can and get in lots of fluids to keep her hydrated as much as possible."

"Ok," I agreed, "I can do that."

"Great, and I'll send you home with some Pedialyte to make sure that Ari is taking in enough electrolytes. The stomach flu is rough on young tummies and worrying for the mamas, that's for sure, but Ari should start feeling better within the next few days, don't worry. If all goes well, I will see you in seven months for her four year visit. But don't hesitate to call if things still aren't going well in a week from now, ok?"

"Yes, ok. Thank you for your help, Dr. Henz. You've definitely eased my worries."

"Good, I'm glad." She touched my shoulder comfortingly. Then she stood up and placed her hand on the door handle.

I glanced over at Ari. Taking on an English accent once again, I said, "Alright, my princess, Ari, are you ready to claim your prize of bravery at the royal guards' desk?"

She sat up and slid off the table in excitement.

"Yes!" she shouted. Then she turned to Dr. Henz and waved.

Dr. Henz smiled, "Alright, baby, goodbye! Feel better, you hear?"

"I will," she said.

Dr. Henz opened the door and, with a wave, walked away.

Unable to wait any longer, Arielle skipped out of the room to the check-out desk to claim a blue raspberry sucker that she immediately stuck in her mouth. She also picked out a cat sticker that said "PAWSITIVELY BRAVE" and stuck it on her knee-cap.

There's my silly, goofy girl! I think she's feeling better already!

I breathed out, relieved, and I smiled.

DEFEAT (ONE WEEK LATER)

I startled awake as I heard the patter of Arielle's little feet run into the bathroom. Arielle had started to have bouts of emesis for a few days now on top of everything else. It had been a week since I had taken her to the pediatrician, and she wasn't getting better. She was much worse.

I sat up and grew nauseous with worry. After hopping out of bed, shuffling into my slippers, and throwing on my robe, I walked quickly to the bathroom. Arielle was on her knees, hunched over the toilet bowl with her hair dangling and some sticking to her mouth. *I had not been quick enough.*

She started to gag again, so I quickly knelt down and held her curls out of the way.

I rubbed her back tenderly. "It's ok, honey, it's ok." I tried to assure her, but I couldn't help but think that everything was definitely not ok.

I grabbed a tissue and wiped her mouth when she seemed like she was done.

She looked up at me. Tears had collected in the corners of her light brown eyes, and her face was red from retching and flushed with fever.

"I'm sorry I got some in my hair, Muma."

"Oh, honey, I'm not mad. I can give you a nice bubble bath when you feel up to it. I just wish you would feel better, sweetie."

"Me too. I don't like feeling yucky."

"I know, honey, I'm sorry."

* * *

The warm water rose and groups of bubbles multiplied quickly. Arielle stood naked in the bathtub, holding a rubber baby doll dressed in a polk-a-dot swimsuit, and waiting for the water to get up to her knees. Only then, was I allowed to turn off the water. She was there to make sure I didn't do it a second sooner.

Her legs and arms seemed thinner to me and her abdomen was distended. Random bruises claimed territory on her lower legs and elbows.

Just two weeks and two days ago, she was healthy—or at least she seemed to be. My eyes became blurry with tears. I was at a loss. I felt defeated. I had researched and tried every possible home remedy to try to heal her body. *Why wasn't the virus clearing up by now? What was I missing?*

It was too late to call Dr. Henz now; I would call her first-thing tomorrow morning.

CHAPTER 4

DOUBLE TROUBLE (THE NEXT DAY)

Sunlight streamed in through the window, casting a pale glow on my chest and stomach. I sat up in bed, feeling nauseous.

The sheets were wrinkled next to me. Ivaan was probably up cooking breakfast since Emilia had to leave for school in an hour. Arielle was most likely awake too. She insisted that she be woken up early during the school week because she liked to walk Emilia to the bus stop with Ivaan each morning.

I slid out of bed. Fuzzy darkness replaced my vision momentarily. The nausea grew more intense. I placed my hand on the bed, steadying myself.

I slowly walked out of the room, down the stairs, and into the hallway. A comforting scene unfolded before me as the hallway ended. Ivan stood at the stove, flipping pancakes—eggs cooking and bacon sizzling in the pans to his left. Arielle and Emilia sat on the white, fluffy rug in front of the couch, giggling and playing with Tilly, our grey tabby kitten.

Everything seemed normal. *Had it all just been a terrible nightmare?*

My question proved to be wishful thinking as I watched Ari stand up. Her distended abdomen jutted out beneath her purple princess nightgown. Anxiety buzzed through me, but I kept walking and put on a smile.

"Good morning, girls!"

"Good morning!" they responded in unison.

I walked up and wrapped my arms around Ivaan's waist, resting my chin on his shoulder. "Good morning, babe," I whispered.

He turned around, smiling and kissing me on the forehead.

The greasy, buttery scent of the breakfast cooking made my mouth water. But it wasn't from hunger, I realized. I ran to the bathroom, kneeling down in front of the toilet just in time. I looked up, coughing, and wiped my mouth with a tissue.

I flushed the toilet, washed my hands, and made my way back out to the kitchen. Ivaan stood at the island, preparing plates for us and the girls. He looked up, concerned.

"Honey, what happened? Are you ok?"

"Yeah," I said hesitantly, "I just threw up. I must be getting whatever Ari has." I paused, then continued, "I mean, I was feeling nauseous yesterday, but I didn't want to jinx it by saying anything. But today I woke up nauseous and lightheaded." I sighed. "Oh boy, I really don't have time for this at all. Ari still isn't feeling well, and I need to call the doctor's office, and my…"

Ivaan touched my shoulder. "Hey, hey," he said softly, "let's just take one thing at a time, honey. Everything is going to be ok."

"But what if it's not?" I said, raising my voice. "What if something is terribly wrong? I mean, look at Ari…she's really sick!" Redness coated my cheeks—partly from frustration, but mostly because I realized I was yelling.

The girls were staring at me, concerned. I rarely ever raised my voice, and Ivaan and I didn't believe in pointless arguing—the type that only served the purpose of overriding silence.

"Everything's ok, girls. Mum is just a little stressed right now. Keep playing with Tilly." Ivaan told them.

I looked Ivaan in the eyes. "Thanks, hon. I'm so sorry. I didn't mean to yell. I'm just so worried about Ari, and I want her to be ok—I need my baby to be ok."

"I know, honey, me too. We're going to figure this out, though, ok?"

I nodded. "We have to."

* * *

My fork scraped against my plate as I shifted the cold eggs and syrup-sogged pancakes around. I couldn't bring myself to eat. I felt physically and emotionally ill.

Ivaan and Arielle had gotten home from walking Emilia to the bus stop about an hour ago. Arielle was napping in my and Ivaan's bed, and Ivaan was taking a shower. He had to leave for work in ten minutes.

I glanced up at the clock. The doctor's office opened in two minutes. Only 120 more seconds, and I could finally call. Today, it seemed as though God had hired a sloth to control the time. I tapped my fingers on the counter, nervously.

The second hand ticked ever so slowly, traveling in a circle two times. A backwards "L" formed on the clock. It was finally 9:00am.

I grasped my cell phone in my hands and dialed the doctor's office phone number. It rang briefly before someone answered.

"Hello, Pediatric Primary Care Center of Cardinal Children's Hospital, Delilah speaking, how may I help you?"

"Hi, Delilah, my name is Norah Ekner, and I'm calling regarding my daughter, Arielle Ekner."

"Alright, may I please have Arielle's birthdate?"

"Yes, it's April 11th, 2014."

"Ok, thank you. What can I help you with, ma'am?"

"Uh, well, about one week ago, I brought Ari in to see her pediatrician, Dr. Henz, because she was having some unusual symptoms. We were told she had a stomach bug and would get better in the next few days. But she has gotten worse and has been vomiting every day, sometimes twice, and her abdomen is distended. She just looks really sick, and I know she feels pretty crappy too. I just have this feeling that something isn't right. Not to mention, I think I'm coming down with whatever Ari has, so that's adding on a bit more stress. But I was just wondering if Dr. Henz could see Ari in clinic soon to reevaluate? I'm just really worried." I paused, eagerly waiting for her to advise.

"Oh, no! I'm so sorry to hear that things have not improved with Ari and that you're sick now as well. I guess it is September; lots of nasty viruses have been going around since school started back up. But give me just a second to let me check Dr. Henz's openings for you."

"Ok, thank you."

Hold music came on—an annoyingly monotonous tone.

Ivaan came rushing into the kitchen, his hair wet and slicked back and a briefcase in his hands. He grabbed an apple from the fruit bowl on the island and blew me a kiss before heading out the garage door to hop in his car and drive off to work. I waved goodbye half-attentively.

The hold music went silent.

"Norah? Are you there?" Delilah checked.

"Yes, I'm listening."

"Ok. I checked her openings, and, unfortunately, the soonest she has is next Friday, the 22nd, at 10:15 in the morning."

I sighed. That was a week from now—a whole seven days. Who knows what condition Ari would be in by then. But there was no other choice.

"Oh, ok. I guess I'll take it. Ah," I placed my hand on my forehead, looking down, "I really wish there was something sooner."

"I'm sorry. If there was, I would surely give it to you. I'll tell you what, I'll call you if there are any cancellations before then that would allow Ari to be seen sooner. And, of course, you can always call our office if there are any major changes or concerns, ok?"

"Yes, ok. Thank you very much, Delilah."

"Yes, of course. My pleasure. You take care."

"Thank you, you too. Goodbye."

"Goodbye."

The disconnect tone sounded.

My eyelids felt heavy, and my body felt shaky. I needed to lie down. Stress and frustration coursed through me as I walked to my bedroom. My body untensed, though, as I saw Arielle napping in the snow angel position. Although her bloated belly still showed when lying flat, everything about her was perfectly precious. She looked so peaceful.

I climbed into bed, taking Ivaan's side. His cologne drifted into my nostrils—earthy and smokey like an autumn woodland. My heart slowed. My body relaxed. I gently grabbed hold of Ari's little hand.

With my daughter resting peacefully beside me, and my husband's comforting scent surrounding me like a familiar embrace, everything felt ok. And I prayed to God that it truly was.

CHAPTER 5

CUE THE ANXIETY (FOUR DAYS LATER)

T he bathroom mirror held a woman with wavy brown hair tied up into a messy bun. Her face was pale, her lips cracked. Her T-shirt was wrinkled and oversized with one side loosely slipping down her shoulder. The woman in the mirror was me. I could hardly recognize myself.

After four sleepless nights, overwhelming stress, and daily vomiting spells, my body had clearly had enough. But being a mom means ignoring your body's limits and forcing it to set new ones in accordance to the nature of a particular situation. So I wasn't going to allow myself to crumble. I couldn't. I had a sick little girl that needed me to stay strong for her. So that's what I was going to do.

As I walked out of the bathroom to head to my room so that I could try to lay back down for a little longer, I heard Ari gagging.

I walked briskly to her room at the opposite end of the hallway. Her room was still dark, but I could see her well enough to not turn on the lights. She was whining, and I could tell that she and her sheets were covered in her stomach contents.

"Oh, honey, don't cry. I'm not mad that you couldn't make it to the bathroom in time," I said, rubbing her back.

She sniffled. "That's not why I'm crying."

"Then what is it, honey? What's the matter?"

"My legs hurt to walk. I tried, Muma, but it hurted too much."

I stood, frozen. I could not believe what my ears had just taken in. *Now my baby couldn't walk? What the hell was going on?* Starting to feel panicky, I took a deep breath in and breathed out slowly. Still, tears gathered in my eyes, and I wanted to scream. But really, I just wanted someone to wake me up from this nightmare or at least hug me and tell me everything would be ok. But no one was there to save me or comfort me. *I have to keep it together for her,* I reminded myself.

I straightened my posture, trying to spur up any life that was left in me. Ivaan's words from yesterday echoed in my mind: *"Everything is going to be ok. We're going to figure this out."*

I finally spoke, "Ari, honey, don't worry. We're going to figure this out, ok? I'm going to call Dr. Henz's office today and find a way to get you feeling better. I promise."

"Ok, Muma. Can you help me get changed into clean pajamas?"

"Of course, honey. What one would you like to wear?" I asked, holding up the options.

She pointed at the leftmost option and smiled. "That one! I love my froggy pajamas!"

"Alright, my silly girl, froggy pajamas it is."

Ari pulled the shirt over her head and poked her arms through the sleeves while I threaded her little legs through the froggy bottoms. She whimpered several times during the process due to my touch aggravating her leg pain.

"Ok, sweetie, let's go to the living room. We can watch some Bluey, and maybe you can get a little more rest. It's still very early."

"Ok, Muma. Can you carry me?"

"Sure, honey. Can you show me how you can't walk first, though?" I impulsively asked. I mean, I believed her; I just found it hard to understand how things had changed so quickly overnight. My eyes wanted to confirm what my ears had heard—what Ari had told me.

"No! Carry me!" she whined.

"Ok, ok, honey. I'm sorry."

She lifted up her arms, reaching for me. I grabbed her small body and shifted her onto my hip. She dangled her legs limply. With one hand, I stripped the sheets off her bed and threw them in the laundry room sink as soon as I got downstairs. I would treat them later.

It was still dark, but getting lighter. I placed Ari on the couch and, from behind her, covered her with her purple blanket. I grabbed the remote and the television flickered on to the episode where Bingo, Bluey's little sister, is in the hospital. Before my thoughts could become obsessively stressed, Ari asked me a question.

"Muma, can I have some apple juice? I'm really thirsty."

"Of course you can, honey. I'll go get you your sippy cup."

I was glad. This was the first time she had asked for any sort of sustenance in days. I walked away and retrieved Ari's pink sippy cup. I filled it with apple juice and brought it back to her. Within the few minutes I was gone, the room had gotten much lighter.

Ari reached out, grabbing the sippy cup from my hands. She started sipping. I looked at her sweet little face, and my heart sank. I turned on the lamp on the table beside her. The space below her left eye was bruised.

"Ari, honey, did you fall and hit your eye or hit it accidentally while playing?" I asked, longing for her to say yes.

"No. Why?" she asked, confused.

"Well, there's a purple bruise under this eye," I explained, pointing. "I'm going to ask Dr. Henz about that, too."

"Muma?"

"What is it honey?"

"Why am I still sick?"

I stared into her sad, innocent eyes, not knowing how to answer her. I simply didn't have an answer. Finally, I said, "I don't know, honey, but I'm hoping Dr. Henz can help us answer that."

She nodded, frowning, and turned forward to continue watching Bluey.

* * *

Four hours had passed. Ari had been resting on the couch for three of them. Ivaan had walked Emilia to the bus stop and was now in the shower. It was 9:02—time to call the office. I headed into my and Ivaan's room, so I wouldn't wake Ari.

I dialed the office's number. Someone picked up instantly on the other end. I could tell it was Delilah's voice. *This would make things easier to explain.*

"Hi, Delilah. This is Norah Ekner. I spoke with you four days ago about my daughter, Arielle Ekner?" I questioned, seeing if she remembered.

"Oh, yes," she confirmed, "Is everything alright, Norah?"

"No, I don't think so. Ari has developed some concerning new symptoms today. I was up early, sick myself, and I went into Ari's room because I heard something. She was crying. She had thrown up in her bed. She said it hurt too much to walk, so she couldn't make it to the bathroom. I cleaned her up and carried her to the living room because she refused to walk. Then, when I turned on the light, I noticed a big purple bruise beneath her left eye, but she denied being hit or falling. All of this really has me worried;

it's all just really strange. I was wondering what Dr. Henz would advise?"

"Oh dear, that is worrying. I'm glad you called. I will get this message to Dr. Henz ASAP, and she will call you back very soon."

"Ok, that sounds perfect. Thank you, Delilah."

"Of course, dear. I wish you and your daughter well."

The disconnect tone filled my ears.

Less than ten minutes later, my phone buzzed. "Hello?" I asked.

"Hi, Norah. This is Dr. Henz."

"Hi, Dr. Henz. Please tell me you have a brilliant plan."

She chuckled briefly. "I don't know if it's a brilliant plan, but I think it's necessary. I heard about everything new going on with Ari, and I agree, it is very concerning. My suggestion at this point is that you take Ari to the emergency department. It doesn't have to be right this second—you can get things situated—but I would advise that you take her in today."

"Ok," I said in understanding. "Dr. Henz, I'm scared."

"I know, darlin'. I'm sorry things are going the way they are. Life isn't fair, that's for sure. But I assure you, honey, Ari will be in good hands. I'll let the ER know you are coming in today, so they know what's going on beforehand, ok?"

"Yes, ok. That sounds good. Thank you, Dr. Henz."

"Alright, honey. You take care now, you hear? You will get through this"

"Ok. I appreciate it. Talk to you later." I hung up the phone, unable to hold my composure any longer. I fell back on the bed and broke down in tears, shaking with strained breaths.

Just then, the bathroom door creaked open. I looked up. Ivaan walked out with a smirk on his face and a towel tied low on his waist. *Gosh, he was adorable, but now was not the time for him to be sexy.*

I continued to wail, unable to calm myself down. Immediately, his demeanor changed. He rushed to my side.

"Norah, honey, what's wrong?"

"Ari...has to go...to the emergency department...Dr. Henz said...to go today." I coughed out in between sobs.

"Oh, God," he said, breathing in deeply and tilting his head back. "Ok, honey, I'm going to call off work and get my sister to pick up Emilia after school."

I nodded, unable to speak. Tears were streaming down my face. I couldn't breathe.

He placed his warm hand on my shoulder, which instantly calmed me down, allowing me to breathe easier.

"Norah," he said, softly, as he gently took my face in his hands and lifted my chin so he could see my eyes, "we're going to get through this."

Breathing in deeply, I nodded. I stood up, closing the space between us. He was still steamy from showering. I rested my tear-stained face on his smooth, water-beaded chest and wrapped my arms around his muscled frame. His heart beat fast, but steady. Although the world seemed to be crumbling around me, I felt safe.

EMERGENCY

Arielle was curled up on my lap. Her head was feverishly warm on my shoulder, and she was whimpering in her sleep. My head rested on Ivaan's shoulder as I watched him quickly fill out the emergency department paperwork.

A small bag rested at my feet and was filled with some essentials as well as some of Ari's favorite things to comfort her while we were here, especially if we had to stay overnight. If we ended up needing anything, though, Ivaan or I could always run back home since we only lived about twelve minutes away from Cardinal Children's Hospital.

The combination of bright overhead lights, sanitary scents, hospital busyness, and colorful pediatric scenery overstimulated my already overwhelmed heart and mind. Even still, my eyes started to droop from exhaustion, which allowed oblivious peace to blanket me momentarily.

I startled awake as Ari slowly sat up, swiveling her head left and right to observe her surroundings. She was clearly confused.

She had only woken up briefly on the ride to the hospital and had never even asked where we were heading.

"Muma, where are we? Where's Em?"

I spoke softly, "Honey, Em's still at school. And we're at the hospital. Dr. Henz told us to take you here because you're still so sick, honey, and we need to get you feeling better. Aunt Indie will pick Em up from school and take her back to her house until we get home—hopefully later today. So don't worry, sweetie, everything will be ok, and Muma and Daddy will be with you the whole time, ok?"

"Ok," she agreed hesitantly.

I hugged her close.

* * *

"Arielle," an ER nurse called out. He was tall and slender in his navy blue scrubs, and he wore a friendly smile on his face.

Finally, I thought with relief. We had been waiting for almost three hours now, and Ari was getting pretty restless. She had asked Ivaan to bring her over to the large fish tank to watch the fish about ten times now.

"Ivaan...Ari," I called out, turning towards the fish tank and motioning them to follow me.

Ivaan hurried over with Ari in his arms and handed the nurse the clipboard of paperwork.

The nurse smiled and gave a nod. "Hello, Mom, Dad, and Arielle. My name is Andrew. The ER has been notified by Dr. Henz of your situation, so things should move fairly efficiently from here on out. Sorry about the wait." He paused, then started to walk forward. "Alright, this way folks. I'm going to get Arielle's vitals and then set you up in a room where the team will come in, take a look, and figure out next steps."

Ivaan and I nodded as we followed behind at a brisk pace.

Decals of underwater ocean life covered the walls completely in the particular hallway we were in.

"Fishey!" Ari exclaimed, pointing dramatically at a clownfish on the wall.

"Yeah!" Andrew said excitedly. "Looks like Nemo! Do you like Nemo, Ari?"

Ari smiled. "Yeah, he's brave!"

"That's right! Bravest fish in the sea—at least that's what he thought until you came swimming along!"

Ari giggled.

My heart felt lighter. It was hard to get Ari to laugh lately, but Andrew seemed to know how to speak her language—no wonder he worked in pediatrics.

I smiled. *Dr. Henz was right: Ari was in good hands.*

After Andrew got Ari's weight and height—which, although in pain, she agreed to stand for—and then temperature and blood pressure, we rounded the corner and entered a dimly lit room. There was a hospital gurney with a white fitted sheet over it and two chairs to the left of it. I set my small bag on one of the chairs.

"Alright, little guppy, how about you sit on the bed for me," Andrew offered.

"Ok, but...I'm not a guppy," Ari said with a hint of sass.

"Oh, my apologies," Andrew recovered. "What brave fish of the sea are you then?"

"The one daddy showed me in the fish tank! I'm an angelfish!"

"Hmmm, Ari the angelfish. I like it! I stand corrected."

Ari grinned. "You're funny!"

"Why thank you! It is part of my clownfish nature after all." He winked.

Ari smiled slightly, not fully understanding the joke, but Ivaan chuckled.

Andrew logged in to the hospital's computer system and charted all he knew about Ari so far. Ivaan gently set Ari on the bed, and I unzipped my small bag, taking out and giving Ari her purple blanket and stuffed unicorn.

"Here you go, honey." I said softly.

She smiled sleepily, and lay back on the upright-positioned bed, clutching her blanket and unicorn close to her abdomen.

"Ok, it looks like everything is now up-to-date in her chart, so all I'm going to do right now before the team comes in is print out a hospital bracelet for Ari and give her a gown and socks to change into."

He typed information quickly into the computer and grabbed a white bracelet with fine print on it from a small machine.

"May I see your wrist Ari? I just have to give you this special bracelet. It helps all of the doctors and nurses in this aquarium know that you are a special fish that's allowed to swim here." He held out his hand expectantly.

Ari placed her forearm in his hand, and he fastened the bracelet around her small wrist.

"Perfect! Now here is your special outfit to wear while you are here; it will make swimming easier." He dropped a mint green gown and a pair of baby blue hospital socks onto the bed. "Alright, I think that should be it for now. Mom, Dad, Ari...do you have any questions?"

There was a brief period of silence. Then, I said, "Not yet, but I'm sure we will."

"That's quite alright. Please don't hesitate to ask when you do. I will be back a little later, I'm sure, but the team should be in within half an hour, ok?"

"Yes, ok. Thank you so much Andrew. I appreciate you making our girl laugh," said Ivaan.

"Oh, my pleasure." His eyes widened and he threw up his pointer finger vertically. "I almost forgot..." He went out and returned in seconds with a white blanket. "I have a special blanket for you!"

Ari looked up at the white blanket in Andrew's hands and then down at her own purple blanket.

Sensing her confusion, Andrew explained, "I got this white blanket from our special blanket warmer, so it will help you stay nice and cozy. I promise, you'll be much more comfortable with two blankets."

Ari nodded, and he placed the warm blanket over her. Ari poked her unicorn's head out at the top end of the blanket out of consideration for her beloved stuffy's quality of breathing, and she smiled her sweet little smile.

CHAPTER 7

STEP ONE

As I helped Arielle change out of her clothes and into the hospital attire, I watched my unwell, but normal-appearing girl transform into a sick little hospital kid. All of the sudden, everything felt very real. It was almost too much to bear. I was experiencing every parent's worst nightmare, and there was no chance that shifting from sleep to wake could save me, Ari, or anyone else.

As we waited for the ER team to come in, Ivaan found Bluey on the hospital's TV for Ari to watch, and I took a moment to pray—for Ari, but also for the nurses, doctors, Ivaan, me, and Em. It's true, things had been especially difficult for Ari since she had gotten sick, but it had also been excruciating for Ivaan and I to helplessly watch Ari get sicker and hard for Em to understand why Ari still doesn't feel well enough to play with her most of the time.

I opened my eyes, startled by the knock on the door.

Ivaan and I looked at each other and then at the door as a team of four doctors walked in. Clothed in their white coats, they held their clipboards firmly in their hands with their heads held high. Their warm smiles and colorful pens clipped in their pockets, however, seemed to neutralize the intimidatingly studious atmosphere at least a little.

A doctor with greying hair stepped forward from the group. "Hello Ivaan, Norah, and Arielle. I'm Dr. Osko, the head ER doctor at Cardinal Children's Hospital, and these are my residents," he said as he motioned to the three doctors behind him. They nodded and smiled in response to his recognition of them. Dr. Osko continued, "We have reviewed Arielle's chart and would like to make sure we're all on the same page before we get started. So would it be ok if we asked you guys a few questions?"

"Of course," Ivaan replied.

Arielle looked around curiously at everyone in the room before focusing her full attention back to the television mounted on the wall, where a blue heeler was trying to keep a red balloon from falling to the ground in a game called "keepy uppy". Ari and Em loved imitating the games that Bluey and Bingo played. It saddened me as I thought of how quiet the house had been lately.

"Excellent," Dr. Osko confirmed. "Now, when did Arielle's symptoms start and what changes were you guys noticing?" He started to conduct a physical exam on Ari while he waited for us to answer.

"We first noticed a change in Ari's energy levels about three weeks ago, I think it was," I started. "She was taking longer naps and just wasn't acting like her usually playful self. Her appetite was not very good either, so Ivaan and I attributed this to her lower energy levels. But then Ari started having stomach pain, which was concerning to us because it was difficult to get her to eat very much before she was in too much pain to continue." I paused, thinking. "There was this particular day—a Sunday after church—that really told us something wasn't right. Ari was playing with her sister, Emilia, when she just fell to her knees. She was tired, weak, pale, and out of breath. I just thought it was because of her not eating much lately, but when we went out to eat for lunch, Ari barely touched her plate and was clearly feeling pretty lousy. So I brought her home instead of going to the park with Ivaan and Em. Once home, Ari had come down with a fever, and she napped for the rest of the day." I paused.

Sensing I was losing momentum, Ivaan took my hand in his and gave a sympathetic nod and smile.

"Norah took her in to see the pediatrician," Ivaan began, "and it was determined that she just had a stomach bug and would likely feel better in a few days. However, a few days later, Ari started to have vomiting episodes as well, and Norah noticed Ari's abdomen was distended. That morning, Norah and I were discussing what to do when Norah ran to the bathroom and threw up as well. Norah seems to have gotten sick from Ari, although her symptoms seem to be less severe. Anyway, Norah made an appointment for Ari to be reevaluated by Dr. Henz this coming Friday because that's the soonest they had, but obviously things took a turn for the worse since we're in the ER now."

I took over, "Yeah, so today, I woke up to find Ari crying in her bed with vomit all over her and her sheets. She was complaining that it hurt too much to walk so she couldn't make it to the bathroom. I cleaned her up and brought her into the living room. It wasn't until I turned on the light that I realized she had a bruise beneath her eye. She denied hitting it or falling. I grew very worried by all of this, so as soon as Dr. Henz's office opened, I called. She told me to bring Ari to the ER today since they wouldn't be able to see Ari for another three days and her symptoms are very concerning and unusual. So, here we are," I finished.

Uninvited tears had collected in my eyes. Ivaan squeezed my hand tighter.

I looked up. The residents were jotting down notes at full speed as if their lives depended on it—*although, maybe Ari's did.*

Dr. Osko nodded, smiling warmly. "Thank you very much for that summary," he said. "It sounds as though you all have had quite a distressing journey already. But we're here to help figure things out and get Ari feeling better. Based on how Ari is presenting, however, I do not think we are dealing with a virus or infection, so we are going to have to run some extensive testing." He took a deep breath in and looked at me. "Now, Norah, how are you feeling? The team and I weren't made aware of you being symptomatic as well."

"Oh, don't worry about me. I've just been nauseated, throwing up, fatigued, and light-headed at times. But, really, I'm fine."

"I hear you, Norah. I know you want us to focus on Ari. But since we are likely going to be admitting Ari to the inpatient floor, I want to make sure you don't have anything contagious that could spread to other patients."

I nodded in agreement.

"Ok, good. Although CHH is a pediatric hospital, what I think we should do first is get a blood and urine sample from both you and Ari—to rule out anything viral for you, Norah, and as standard protocol for Ari. Does that sound ok?"

I nodded.

Dr. Osko turned and opened a drawer below the sink. He pulled out two cups with orange lids, stuck a white label on each of them, and handed them to me.

"Ok, Norah, if you would help Ari with this and bring both of yours back and put them on the counter, I will get Nurse Andrew to come in and collect a tube of blood from both of you. And then, depending on those results, we'll go from there. Alright?"

"Ok," I agreed.

I looked at Ari and frowned. My poor girl was about to get poked. Ivaan would have to hold her still. She would not be very happy for the rest of the day; I could already tell.

CHAPTER 8

TESTING

Ari and I returned to her room. Ivaan and Nurse Andrew were talking. I placed the two cups on the counter, and set Ari back on her hospital bed.

Nurse Andrew pulled up to Ari's bedside on a stool with a bunch of medical supplies in hand. For Ari, I dreaded what was about to happen next.

"Alright," Nurse Andrew started, "we are going to make this as quick and painless as possible, I promise." He smiled and handed Ari a Nemo stuffed animal. "Are you ready to show Nemo how brave you are, Ari the angelfish?"

Fearful and bashful all at once, Ari scrunched into a ball and covered her face with the Nemo stuffed animal.

"Oh, don't worry. I've got a little friend to help us out!" he said as he pulled out a device in the shape of a bumblebee with a smiley face. "This is Buzzy! He helps make pokes less scary."

Ari looked up and smiled slightly. Nurse Andrew gently took Ari's arm in his hand and fastened Buzzy around her upper arm.

He turned the device on, and it made a buzzing noise from the constant vibrations.

Ari laughed. "That tickles!"

Nurse Andrew smiled. "Good! That means Buzzy is doing his job!"

I watched as the sharp needle slid beneath her pale skin and into a blue vein. Distracted by both Buzzy and the Nemo stuffie, Ari hardly flinched. Blood filtered into the plastic tubing and dripped slowly into a blood collection tube.

A few seconds later, Nurse Andrew said, "All done! Mom's turn now." With his long legs, he awkwardly scooted around Ari's bed and rolled over to me to collect a sample.

* * *

A radiology technician with curly blonde hair stood over Ari. Ari giggled as the tech spread warm gel onto Ari's distended abdomen. Using the sonogram on the ultrasound computer as her guide, she gently navigated the ultrasound probe over the entire surface of Ari's abdomen.

Ari's giggles and the tech's clicking of keyboard keys to capture the images were the only sounds in the room, although *I* could hear the rapid beating of my heart quite loudly.

Ari was doing so well with everything so far, and I was so proud of her, but it couldn't help the fact that I was an untameable nervous wreck.

Flashbacks of my last ultrasound when I was pregnant with Arielle flooded my mind. The strangeness of watching my three-year-old daughter have a medical test that I naively assumed she wouldn't need for another 20 years or so set me on edge. My hands were cold and sweaty. My chest felt tight. My left leg bounced up and down. Ivaan placed his warm, sturdy hand on my thigh in an attempt to calm me. I smiled and breathed out a little easier, but all of the terrible possibilities continued to haunt my mind.

My eyes traveled up to the IV bag of saline fluid hanging on the IV pole beside Ari's bed. I followed the tubing all the way down to Ari's small hand where it was secured with clear dressing. My heart ached, as I remembered how the placement of the IV went. There were a lot of tears as Ivaan held her still and Nurse Andrew struggled to get the IV into her weak dehydrated veins. It was so much more chaotic than the blood draw had been.

At this point, anything and everything was unpredictable.

I wouldn't dare hold my breath.

CHAPTER 9

THE BEST AND WORST (THE NEXT DAY)

It was six o'clock in the morning; we had been at the hospital for 19 hours. In that time, Ari had had a physical exam, urine and blood collected, an IV placed, an abdominal ultrasound done, and heart monitor electrodes stuck to her chest. All of that took about 10 of the 19 hours; the other nine have been for sleeping, or, in my case, stressing and waiting for the doctors to make their seven o'clock morning rounds to deliver the results and next steps.

Arielle was curled up in her purple blanket, with her unicorn stuffed animal wrapped securely in her arms. Her head rested on Ivaan's chest. Ivaan laid on the small gurney awkwardly—half on, half off. It didn't seem to bother him, though. He and Arielle slept soundly.

Although the door was closed and the curtain was drawn, I could still hear the busy commotion of doctors and nurses shuffling past in the hallways. A child would cry or scream every now and then. Monitors were beeping almost all of the time—set off by any stat that strayed from the machine's sensitive settings. The ER was a highly alert environment. It had to be. Anything and everything was unpredictable.

* * *

My heart beat faster as I heard the hand sanitizer dispenser right outside of the door go off multiple times. Dr. Osko and his residents knocked and entered the cubicle-sized room. They still wore warm smiles, but there was a hint of sympathy in their eyes.

What? What had they found? I longed to know, yet I wished there was nothing for them to tell. I wished the present scene would just crumple to the ground, and I would wake up from this awful nightmare at last. But, no matter how hard I tried, I would not; I would have to live through it. It was a nightmare in the flesh, not fantasy. I sighed, trying to mentally prepare myself for whatever they had to say.

"Ivaan...Norah," Dr. Osko began, "would it be ok if we go out and talk to you in the hallway? There may be some sensitive information that you may not be ready to share with Ari quite yet."

I looked over at Ari. She was peacefully coloring in a Bluey coloring book that a child life specialist had brought her. Her bottom lip jutted out in concentration.

I would have to be strong for her; there was no other choice.

"Ok," I said.

"Yeah, sure," Ivaan agreed.

We both looked at each other nervously as we followed Dr. Osko and his team into the hallway. Ivaan took hold of my hand in a firm grasp. *We were in this together. We would both be strong for Ari.*

Dr. Osko and his colleagues turned around to face Ivaan and me. He smiled slightly before he spoke. "I can imagine that what I'm about to say next will initiate a range of emotions. And that's ok. Don't be afraid to feel them right away. We're here to support.

Now, would you like me to explain Ari's results first or yours, Norah?"

I didn't hesitate, "Please, start with Ari. I don't care what's wrong with me; I need to know what's wrong with our little girl."

Ivaan nodded and waited intently for an explanation.

"Alright, very well." He looked at us with his soft, serious eyes and cleared his throat before continuing, "Arielle's blood test shows anemia, which means her body isn't making enough blood cells to support her body's needs. In her case, however, her anemic state is not due to a blood disorder."

"I don't understand. What's causing it then?" Ivaan asked, his voice a little too loud.

He was frustrated and scared. I could tell. I smoothed my hand up his muscular arm. It was the least I could do; I knew I would probably be losing it, myself, in a few seconds.

Dr. Osko breathed in deeply, "Well, in combination with the high levels of catecholamines in her blood and urine and the tumor-like mass that the ultrasound revealed, we believe that Arielle may be suffering from neuroblastoma, which is a rare type of cancer."

Midway into a breath, I stopped—froze. Then, my hand slid down Ivaan's arm, and I fell to my knees.

"My baby has cancer?" I sobbed out. "My baby has cancer...no, no, no, no...this can't be happening! THIS CAN'T BE HAPPENING!" I yelled. My elbows fell to the floor, and I caught my head in my hands as my tears melted me into a puddle on the floor.

Ivaan crumpled down beside me and wrapped his arms around my middle. He was shaking from sobbing as well.

One word had broken both of us. We had no muscles, no bones, no strength. We could feel nothing. We could hear nothing. Nothing existed except a terrible emotional pain in our hearts—stabbing us until we couldn't remember how to breathe or think or move.

***

Ivaan had recovered first, and then I.

Somehow, Dr. Osko and his colleagues had managed to reassemble us back into human form, and we were now sitting in chairs. Ivaan was slumped back lazily, unable to put forth any effort towards his posture. But I was stiffly straight-backed from anxiety.

A distraught look claimed my face, and it wouldn't leave. *Arielle had cancer. My sweet baby had cancer.* Nothing could have prepared me to hear those words. Nothing at all.

After a few minutes of silence, Dr. Osko spoke, "I am extremely sorry that these were the results I had to relay to you regarding Ari. I truly wish I had better news. But I do want you guys to understand that we will not give up on Ari; we remain optimistic at CCH until improvement is made—which is the hope—or until nothing else can be done. I promise you, Ari is in excellent hands."

"Thank you, Dr. Osko. We appreciate the confidence and support," Ivaan said.

All I could manage was a nod.

"Before we finalize treatment plans, however, and have the consultant pediatric oncologist come speak to you both, we want to run one more test. The anemia, bruising around her eye, high levels of catecholamines, and all of her other symptoms all point to neuroblastoma, but the mass found on the ultrasound was inconclusive. We want to have Ari undergo an MIBG scan, which is a special scan that helps to diagnose and stage cancers like neuroblastoma. I believe this test will help us gather more information about the extent of Ari's condition, so we know how to treat her more effectively and on an individualistic level."

"Wait," Ivaan interrupted, "are you saying that there is a possibility that Ari may not even have cancer?"

"No, not exactly," Dr. Osko replied. "Ari does have cancer, but the ultrasound alone was not comprehensive enough to allow us to give her a proper diagnosis. We need to do the MIBG scan in order to evaluate the stage of her cancer and see where it originated and if there is any spread. A little later today, I will come back with some radiology and nuclear medicine staff to explain how the scan works, so don't worry about that right now."

We both nodded. I was starting to feel a little more composed, but everything still felt surreal. *Like, this is my daughter—my baby—that we're talking about.*

Dr. Osko sensed the atmosphere becoming calmer as we talked. "Please know that this is completely up to you guys, but would you like me to go over your results, Norah? I know it's been a lot to take in and process already, so I understand if you would rather wait."

Ivaan and I looked at each other. His eyes stared longingly into mine. He wanted me to decide.

"I guess you can tell us now," I said. "It can't possibly get any worse. Besides, I really can't handle anymore waiting; it will drive me crazy."

"Ok, I will tell you then," said Dr. Osko. "Your blood test results came back normal, so I have no concerns about you having a virus or infection since your white blood cell count wasn't high. Your urine test, however, shows high levels of human chorionic gonadotropin. In other words, Norah, your fatigue, lightheadedness, nausea, and vomiting spells have all been signs of morning sickness. Norah, you're pregnant."

My hands flew up to my gaped-open mouth, and my eyes widened. I felt Ivaan hug me, but I didn't know whether to cry or laugh or scream or run or jump up and down. Maybe I would do everything all at once. *How had I not realized I was pregnant?* I guess maybe because I hadn't experienced morning sickness with my other two pregnancies, or maybe because I got sick around the same time as Ari, or maybe because I thought stress was to blame for me skipping my last cycle.

Whatever the case, I had just received the best and worst news of my life all at once, and I was certainly not amused by the timing of it all.

CHAPTER 10

THE SCAN

It was now four in the afternoon, and Ari was due to go up to radiology for her MIBG scan anytime now.

Nurse Taylor, who had taken over for Nurse Andrew, had already injected the iodine-131-metaiodobenzylguanidine (MIBG) through her IV hours ago so that it would have enough time to be absorbed by any cancerous cells in Ari's body and then light up on the scan. The scan would last up to two hours, so Ari would have to be given anesthesia in order to remain still for that long.

Since we came to the ER yesterday morning, Ari had not had anything to eat or drink other than small sips of water and apple juice. She had gotten so sick so fast. I still couldn't wrap my mind around this cruel reality. I didn't even really know what half the words Dr. Osko had mentioned this morning even meant. But we would be having a meeting with the consultant pediatric oncologist later today once Ari's MIBG scan results were in, so I'm sure I would find out soon enough.

We were still in the emergency department since a room hadn't opened up on the inpatient floor yet. *Hopefully one would soon, though.* We could all use our own, quiet space that had a window with the sun shining in. This emergency room was becoming way too depressing.

Nurse Taylor knocked and entered Ari's room. In the hallway, stood a small wheelchair. *Radiology must be ready for Ari.*

"Hi, Ari! Are you ready to take a little ride up to the third floor?" she asked, smiling. She pushed her brown, curly hair behind her shoulder and placed her hand on her hip.

Ari looked up, hesitant.

"It's ok, sweetie," Ivaan assured her. "They said you can bring your blanket and unicorn with you, and Muma and I will be waiting right here for you when you're done. You'll be taking a nice nap, too, so nothing will hurt, honey."

Ari reached her hands up to Ivaan. He picked her up and placed her in the small wheelchair out in the hallway. Before turning back around, he bent down to give her a hug. I walked over and kissed the top of Ari's head. *This may be one of the last times my lips touch her radiantly curly hair for a while—treatment would leave peach fuzz at the very most.*

We watched as Nurse Taylor wheeled Ari away.

I hardly looked at Ivaan as he sat down. There was no point; I had no smile to give and no words to say.

We sat in silence. I assumed he felt utterly empty inside too. There was just nothing to give. Not right now.

* * *

An hour had passed. Only a few sentences had been exchanged between Ivaan and I. Ivaan had stepped out of the room a few minutes ago. Usually we talked through the hard things with each other; it was natural for us. And we still would, I knew, but this situation was different. This unspeakable grief demanded silence first.

Ivaan came back into the room with two cups of water. He handed one to me.

"Thanks," I said, only slightly smiling.

"Nor," Ivaan started, "Indie wants to Facetime us tonight. She said Em's been asking her to do so almost every hour."

I nodded. Then I placed my elbows on my knees and my face in my hands.

"Ivaan, I don't know how to tell her. I don't know how to tell her that her little sister has cancer. I mean, Ari's three—she won't care to know everything. But Em's almost eight. She's going to have questions. She's going to want to know the whole truth."

"I know, honey. I was thinking that too. I mean, I think we're just going to have to tell everything to Em as simply as possible. It's going to be difficult, I know, but I think she deserves to know the whole truth. She should know what will happen to her sister and what could happen. I don't think it's fair to keep *that* from her."

As much as I wanted to disagree, he was right. *We can't pretend that an uncertain future for Ari doesn't exist.*

"Yeah, you're right. Em's old enough to understand the seriousness of the situation. We'll just have to tell her all of the medical stuff in simpler terms."

Ivaan nodded and looked down at my middle section.

What? Was my bra showing? Was there a stain on my shirt?

I looked down at my shirt. And then it struck me. *Right, I was pregnant. There was that to tell too.*

I chuckled and placed my hands on my abdomen. "Right...this...I suppose we're going to have to sprinkle that into the conversation as well."

He smiled charmingly. "Hey, how far along do you think you are?"

"Gosh, I don't know...six to eight weeks maybe?"

"Wow, that's crazy. I didn't even think of that when you told me about your nausea and everything."

"Yeah, me neither. It was definitely a complete surprise. After we had Ari...I don't know...I guess I kind of thought we were done having kids. But I guess God had other plans." I laughed and laid my head on Ivaan's shoulder.

"Yeah, He definitely did. But...He'll help us get through them. For now, think of our situation like a bomb that explodes confetti." He smirked and turned to kiss my forehead.

I smiled at his cleverness. But my anxiety triggered a thought.

I hope he's right. I hope there's confetti at the end of all of this. I hope we aren't hitting blindly at a pinata full of explosives.

CHAPTER 11

THE CONSULT (THE NEXT DAY)

Dr. Osko and his colleagues and Dr. Tallon, the consultant pediatric oncologist, sat in an arch around the circular desk. Papers were scattered out in front of them. Ivaan and I sat across from them, a bubble of anxiety enveloping us both. Ivaan's hands were folded and resting on the desk in front of him. My hands were clasped together and buried between my knees to keep them from shaking.

The consult room had a window, but only bloated grey clouds dressed the sky. It looked as if it might storm. *Even the heavens above had absorbed our sadness; we, alone, couldn't contain it all.*

Dr. Osko cleared his throat. "I'm going to start by going a bit more in-depth about what we discussed earlier this morning. Now that you have faced the initial shock of it all, I think the details will help your brains make more sense of what's really happening. After that, Dr. Tallon will share Ari's MIBG scan results and explain what everything means."

Ivaan and I nodded, and silence filled the room momentarily before Dr. Osko continued.

"As I said this morning, Ari's blood and urine sample both showed elevated catecholamine levels. Catecholamines act as both hormones and neurotransmitters that help maintain the body's natural state of function. Dopamine, norepinephrine, and epinephrine are examples of catecholamines that you may be familiar with. Stress, certain medications, and, in Ari's case, cancer can cause these levels to rise. The neuroblastoma cells in Ari's body are secreting these at a rapid rate because they lack the ability to store them for later use. Her body is metabolizing these molecules as they are secreted, so that's why we see excess amounts of catecholamine metabolites in her urine and blood. This is a very common abnormality with neuroblastoma because it is a neuroendocrine cancer, which means all of the organs that produce hormones and those that control electrical signals sent to and from the brain are significantly affected."

He paused, making sure we were still with him. Then he continued.

"Ari's blood test also showed anemia, which means her body isn't producing enough healthy blood cells at a quick enough rate to sustain her body's needs. Treatment for neuroblastoma will cause the body to struggle to produce blood cells, but since Ari has not yet had any treatment, her anemia is likely due to the fact that cancerous cells are invading her bone marrow. Being that bone marrow is basically the blood cell factory of the body, Ari's ability to make her own blood is already severely compromised. In combination with treatment, her bone marrow will struggle even more to do its job, so, unfortunately, blood transfusions will likely need to become pretty regular for Ari while she's in active treatment."

He paused, searching our eyes for any confusion. Finding only grief, he went on.

"In regards to Ari's ultrasound, a mango-sized lump was found above her left kidney and was also palpable upon physical examination. The ultrasound also showed other areas of concern for tumor growth, but the images were not clear enough to tell for certain, so that's why we ordered the MIBG scan."

He turned to Dr. Tallon. She adjusted her glasses and shuffled some papers around in her frail, veiny hands.

"Are you ready for me to continue?" she asked. Her voice was soft. "I know how overwhelming it can be to have so much uninvited information thrown at you."

Ivaan and I stared briefly into each other's eyes.

"I think we're ok," Ivaan decided.

"Ok," she said. She licked her lips before speaking again. "Ari's MIBG scan has a curie score of 27. A curie score is used to help stage neuroblastoma and ranges from zero to 30—zero being no evidence of disease and 30 being...well, detection of significant and extensive disease. So, with a score of 27, this labels Ari's cancer as Stage 4 High Risk Neuroblastoma, which means cancerous cells have metastasized, or spread, all over her body. Her kidneys, liver, lymph nodes, orbits, bones, and bone marrow all lit up on the scan. The mango-sized tumor that Dr. Osko had mentioned was the largest and brightest area that lit up on the scan. Therefore, we suspect that is where the cancer originated—in the immature nerve cells of her adrenal gland, right above her left kidney. The 'high risk' portion of Ari's diagnosis means that even if Ari does go into remission after treatment, there is an extremely high chance of relapse, which means her cancer could come back."

She paused, swallowing, and looking up at us.

Significant and extensive disease. Stage 4. High risk. Metastasized. All over her body. Mango-sized tumor. Extremely high chance of relapse. Cancer could come back. All of these terrible, nightmarish words swirled around in my mind, creating a tortuous tornado.

But one snippet of the conversation echoed louder than the rest: '*even if*'.

I didn't think my heart could possibly break anymore, but grief had made it fragile. I lost all composure and let out a strangled cry as I felt it shatter into a million pieces.

CHAPTER 12

LIKE A FIREFLY

Emilia's sweet voice sounded through Ivaan's iphone. *Oh, what my ears have missed these past two days.* She was skipping and twirling around in her pink tutu and singing along to the music in the background.

"So, honey, did you have fun at ballet class last night?" Ivaan asked.

"Emmhmm," Em replied, trying not to lose her focus. "This is my favorite part! Watch!"

She flung out her arms to her sides and curtsied, dainty, before jumping up and landing as the music stopped.

"Good job, my little ballerina!" I applauded.

"Yay!" Ari shouted, clapping.

"Thank you, fans! Thank you, Thank you!" Em exclaimed, bowing dramatically several times. She laughed and stuck her face into the camera, sticking out her tongue.

Ari giggled. "Hey!"

"Come on, honey, back up a bit," Indie gently scolded Em.

Em backed away, frowning. "I miss you, Ari."

"Miss you too, Em."

"And so do Mum and Dad," I added.

"When are you going to be home?" Em complained.

"I'm not sure, sweetie. But it probably won't be for awhile. You can come visit on the weekend or one day after school, though. And Dad will be coming home in a couple of days because of work."

"Ok. Mum..." she said, hesitating to continue, "is Ari going to be ok?"

I paused, not knowing how to answer. *I should just tell her. Now. Just rip the band-aid off.*

"Honey, we need to share something tough with you. Ari doesn't know this yet, either. We just figured it would be better if we told you both at the same time."

"Ok, what's wrong?" Em asked, waiting.

I turned to Ivaan. He had offered to do the hard part; I knew I wouldn't be able to get far before choking up. Indie smiled sympathetically and gave a nod of encouragement. Ivaan had called to tell her earlier. We had also decided it would be best to avoid the baby part right now. We didn't want to distract from the immediate issue and overwhelm the kids. Plus, I wasn't that far along; it would be a minute before I even started to show.

Ivaan breathed in deeply. "Em, you know how we went to the park that day after brunch and Ari and Mum went back home?"

I didn't know where he was going with this, but I trusted him.

"Yeah, why?" Em responded.

"Well, do you remember asking me about the little boy on the swing?"

"Yeah, he was bald. You said he had cancer. His dad told you." She paused, trying to understand. "Wait, does Ari have cancer?" Her brown eyes were serious.

Ivaan began, "Yes, honey. She has—"

"I don't understand! Ari's not bald like that boy was!" She interrupted, looking worried and confused.

"Honey, cancer didn't make that little boy bald; it's because of the medicine he has to take to get better."

"Oh." Em's shoulders slumped. "So Ari's going to lose her hair? We won't be able to play hair salon anymore?"

"Yes, Ari is probably going to lose her hair, honey. Ari has a lot of bad cells in her body that the doctors are going to try hard to get rid of."

I looked at Ari. She was being quiet, but I wasn't sure how much she was actually understanding.

"But how do the doctors know she has cancer if she's not bald yet?" Em asked, still not fully understanding.

"They did a test that took special pictures of Ari's body and found bad cells everywhere."

"But how did they know?" questioned Em.

In her little mind, I knew she was trying hard to turn the situation around, trying to find where the mistake had been made. But I also knew she wouldn't be able to.

"Well, in the pictures, all of the bad cells lit up."

"Oh. Like a Christmas tree?"

Ivaan nodded. "Yeah, kind of like a—"

"Like a firefly!" Ari chimed in, smiling.

"Yeah, honey, like a firefly," I said. I was glad that she couldn't sense the seriousness of it all; she was too young for that kind of stress. The more normal we kept things, the better. Because a whole lot was about to change.

A tear slipped down my cheek and onto Ari's hand, right next to her IV.

Noticing, Ari said, "Don't worry, Muma, God loves fireflies. God gave fireflies light so they aren't scared when it's dark."

CHAPTER 13

TRIPLE C (THE NEXT DAY)

Dr. Osko and Dr. Tallon stood with clipboards gripped firmly in their hands and stethoscopes draped loosely around their necks. After spending nearly 50 hours in the ER, they had just informed us that there was finally an open bed on the inpatient floor.

"That's great!" Ivaan exclaimed. "What floor will we be on?"

"Well, since Ari is a pediatric oncology patient due to start treatment on Monday, she will be on the seventh floor, which is also known as the Cardinal Cancer Center or, more commonly, Triple C. The whole floor is dedicated to our pediatric oncology kiddos and their families so that transportation to other floors for testing and treatments is almost never necessary. We have a bed ready for her in room 27."

"That will be very nice," Ivaan commented.

"Yeah, that's nice," I said, detached.

I looked down at Ari sleeping peacefully on the gurney. Her cheeks were flushed. Her pale lips were parted slightly.

"Would it be alright if we had Nurse Kali from Triple C bring Ari up now?" Dr. Osko asked.

"Yes, that would be great. I think we are all ready to have our own space." Ivaan replied.

I nodded. "But I hate to wake her," I interjected.

"No worries," said Dr. Tallon. "We can bring her up on the gurney, so she can continue to rest."

"Ok," I agreed. I smoothed back Ari's hair and softly kissed her curly-haired head.

* * *

Nurse Kali pushed Ari on a gurney ahead of us. We walked down the hallways of Triple C. A lot of the doors, walls, and windows we passed were covered with patient artwork. That's not what held my attention, though.

With every patient room we passed, I instinctively peered briefly into the windows—catching only a glimpse of the hell each patient and family were going through.

A baby girl sat in a hospital crib. She was completely bald and lacked eyebrows and eyelashes. Her eyes were sunken and her skin dark from dehydration and treatment. Big, blue veins claimed her temples. Wires and tubing resided all over her chest. She gave a passionate baby laugh as a lady, who I assumed was her mother, tickled her belly.

So young. So innocent. So burdened, yet so happy.

A teenage boy sat upright in a hospital bed. His hair was still thick and plentiful. He was shirtless and his ribs were protruding. A deep red scar curved across his abdomen. A bright yellow bag of chemotherapy and a bag of blood hung on an IV pole beside him. The tubing traveled into a port in his chest. The glow from a computer on his lap reflected in his glasses.

So young. So innocent. So alone, yet so fearless.

A little boy lay in a hospital bed. His face was flushed and his body bloated from treatment. His eyes were closed, and there was a stiff tube poking out of his mouth. Sounds of swishing air pumped into the tube from a machine that was helping him breathe. Several adults, who I assumed were the boy's family, were either laying next to him and clutching his hand or hunched over him, crying. A doctor stood by the ventilator.

So young. So innocent. So fragile, yet so strong.

A little girl with dark skin and hair sat in a hospital chair, crying. A nurse tried to approach her calmly with a butterfly needle and a small syringe of medicine. The little girl screamed harder, pushing herself into the cushioned back of the chair—desperately trying to escape the needle that would inevitably have to poke into the port in her chest.

So young. So innocent. So distressed, yet so brave.

All of these patients were different, but all of them were fighting the same fight. And my little girl had been drafted to join them.

PART 2: FLY AND FEND
_____

Three months later...

CUTTING CURLS

I neatly placed five days worth of items in a bag. Starting on Christmas day—of all days—Ari would be admitted to a room on Triple C to endure her fourth round of intensive chemotherapy. In total, she would need eight rounds before they even attempted surgery to remove the mango-sized lump above her left kidney. I could only hope it was much smaller by now and would be even smaller by then.

March 19th still seemed very far away. And even once Ari reached that day and completed all eight rounds of induction chemotherapy and surgery, treatment would still be far from over. At that point, only phase one would be complete. Then came the even-more-intensive phase two: consolidation. Ari's post-consolidation MIBG scan would need to have a curie score of 0 for her to continue with the treatment plan. This means she would need to be cancer free by the end of phase two to be able to start the final phase of her 18-month long treatment: maintenance chemotherapy.

It was all so overwhelming to think of all at once, so I tried to stay present as much as I could. But with hours and hours of sitting in a hospital watching my child grow weaker from treatment, it was almost inevitable that my mind would obsessively wander and rarely return.

Suddenly, Emilia came running into my room, sniffling, and holding something in her hands.

My eyes grew concerned. "Honey, what's wrong?"

She slowly lifted her fingers away from her palms, revealing a clump of curly, golden hair. *Ari's hair.*

"I was rubbing her head to help her fall asleep," she explained, a tear rolling down her cheek.

About five weeks after treatment began, Ari's hair started to fall out. It was slow at first, but after her third cycle of chemotherapy, it had begun to fall out in clumps. Ari thought it was strange, but she seemed bothered by the uncomfortableness of it all more than any emotions. For Emilia, though, watching her little sister lose her hair had proved to be very upsetting—as had all of the other changes that cancer had brought.

I embraced her, releasing to her all the comfort I could offer.

"It's ok, honey," I whispered into her ear. "Remember, it's happening because the medicines are working hard to get rid of all of the bad cells in Ari's body. And that's a good thing, even though it may seem scary right now." I kissed the top of her head.

She nodded, still deeply upset.

An idea sparked into my mind. "Come here, honey."

I took her hand in mine and led her down the hallway and stairs and into the kitchen. I gripped a handle and pulled open a drawer.

"Here, honey," I said, handing her a plastic, snack-sized bag. "Why don't you take the hair that is in your hand right now and put it in the bag. I'm going to give you a small square of paper, and I want you to write how cancer makes you feel on the front and your prayer for Ari on the back. I know it's hard seeing your sister sick, honey, but I want you to give all of your worries to God, ok? Because 'whenever [you're] afraid,—"

"'...I put my trust in Him'," she finished, her eyes wide and sad but slightly hopeful.

"That's right, Em. That way, whenever you are struggling with sad feelings about Ari and cancer, you can look at this bag and be reminded that there is hope. The God that gave Ari life in her blood and hair on her head, is the same God that can give her the will to fight and help her hair grow back."

She nodded, smiling slightly. "Thanks, Muma. I love you."

"I love you, too, Em. Always and forever." I paused, handing her a small square of paper. "When Dad gets home from work, honey, he's going to shave off the hair that's left on Ari's head. It's becoming too painful and itchy for Ari. Plus, it's easier to do it this way than to keep having clumps fall out. I think that's too emotional for everyone," I said, placing my hand on her shoulder.

She nodded, carefully stuffing Ari's hair into the bag. She took a permanent marker from the side counter, wrote Ari's name in capital bubble letters, and drew a heart on the bag. Then, she scribbled small letters on the paper square and—knowing I was expecting—stepped close to kiss my stomach before running back to Ari's room to check on her.

Her new thing was playing nurse with Ari. *She must like to make herself feel helpful and in control in situations that only God can touch. I could only guess because I often feel the same exact way.*

* * *

Ivaan held a razor in his hand. His bicep flexed as he raised the razor up to the thick, brown hair on his head. He pressed the razor down until it was just one millimeter above his scalp, and he ran it down the center of his head. Then, he looked at the girls and pretended to play a guitar like a rock musician.

Emilia and Ari giggled.

"Dad, you look silly!" Em observed, rolling her eyes playfully.

"Are you kidding? I look awesome!" Ivaan replied, laughing.

Ivaan continued to shave the rest of his hair until his head was smooth. He hovered the razor above his left eyebrow. The girls screamed. I had agreed that he could shave his head to support and encourage Ari and to attempt to make the process less upsetting for Emilia, but I had made it clear that he had to keep his eyebrows. He was the type of guy that would do anything for his family.

He quickly threw down his hand with the razor in it. "I would, but Mum said no," he said and winked at me.

I smiled, thankful. The girls gave out playful sighs of relief and giggled.

"Alright, Ari," Ivaan started, "are you ready to look really cool like me?"

"Ok." She hopped onto the chair, standing, wearing only a pair of princess underwear.

Her legs had gotten stronger with several physical therapy visits, and she was able to walk short distances with less pain. I was so happy about that. But all of the other changes cancer had brought turned me a bit blue.

Ari had a small scar over the left side of her lower abdomen. They had laparoscopically removed her left ovary and freezed some of its ovarian tissue for later implantation, so she could still have the ability to reproduce one day. Treatment would have made her infertile, otherwise. That was surgery number one.

She had a port-a-catheter inserted on the left side of her chest. It looked like a small lump under her skin. It was the most standard way to deliver fluids, medications, and blood to the body during cancer treatment. That way, she'd be able to avoid constant needle pokes throughout each week of treatment; with a port, she only had to be poked—or accessed—once. That was surgery number two.

She had a nasogastric feeding tube. The end of it was stickered to her cheek from which it trailed into the left side of her nose and went all the way down to her stomach. With the large tumor in her abdomen, it wasn't very easy for her to consume adequate amounts of nutrition and fluids, and the chemotherapy often made her sick, so this tube gave her the fuel and hydration her body needed to stay strong and fight.

As I observed all of the visible impacts of the festering cancer in her body, it pained me to realize that this was just the beginning of her cancer making itself known.

Her cancer would only become more high-profile after the next ten minutes I thought as Ivaan took the razor to her head and started shaving.

CHAPTER 15

CHRISTMAS DAY THE CANCER WAY (FOUR DAYS LATER)

I watched as Emilia pushed Ari in her small, purple wheelchair. She had requested to do so. They both had Santa hats on. I hiked a couple feet behind, a few bulky bags in my hands. Since Emilia was off of school for Christmas Break, she had decided to tag along and spend the week with Ari and I at the hospital. We entered the hospital lobby, where a tall Christmas tree stood in the middle—festive but lonely-looking. Paper snowflakes were hung all over the windows—beautiful but stuck and motionless. It was a valiant effort by hospital staff to recreate a Christmas morning atmosphere that anyone at the hospital would be missing. Maybe it satisfied the children, but for the parents, sadness infested everything.

Sure, we had been lucky enough to have a 20-minute Christmas at our house before coming to CCH and before Ivaan had to go to work. But that was only enough time for the kids to look at their stockings and open their big gift from Santa Clause. There were traditions that wouldn't be carried out on their regular date. And there were still quite a few gifts underneath the Christmas tree—although less than previous years because, with the extra expense of Ari's treatments, money was tight. The fact that I wasn't able to get the girls their usual supply of presents didn't bother me, really. They had enough toys; our house practically looked like Toys R Us. What maddened me was the fact that I had to pay extravagant amounts in order for my daughter to even receive treatment for her aggressive cancer. If I had no money to offer, there would be no chance of her surviving; she would just die once the cancer overtook every cell in her little body. *Like, if I want my baby girl to even have a chance at a full life then I have no other choice than to empty my pockets. Gosh, money creates an absolutely twisted prognosis: pay nothing and death is for certain or pay much and death is only possible.*

"Mum! Take a picture of me and Ari!" Em exclaimed.

"Alright, sweetie, go in front of the Christmas tree."

Em wheeled Ari over. Em posed, with her left arm slanted up in the air and her right arm wrapped around Ari. Ari leaned sideways and wrapped her arms around Emilia's waist.

"Ok, say 'Christmas tree!'" I said. And they smiled while I snapped a picture with my iphone.

* * *

Nurse Kali was in again today. She had become one of Ari's favorite nurses. I watched as she slid a butterfly needle into Ari's port. With her face painted with fear, Ari whimpered and flinched back just a little. This was a major improvement from when Ari started treatment. I was so proud of her, but at the same time, I was so unbearably sad for her. Getting poked in the chest with a needle hadn't just become tolerable, it had become normal for her.

"Good job, Ari! You're more brave every time I see you!" Nurse Kali exclaimed.

Ari smiled bashfully.

"Alright, kiddo, let's get you started on your chemo for the day," she said as she connected tubing from a chemotherapy IV bag to Ari's port.

Even though she had seen it done multiple times already, Ari watched intently at everything Nurse Kali was doing. Emilia did too; she was fascinated by this medical world she had stepped into.

"Ok, everything's all set! Do any of you need anything right now? Of course, I'll be back to check on Ari and get vitals shortly."

I looked over at the girls.

"No, I think we're fine right now. Thank you, Nurse Kali." I smiled.

"Of course! Alright then, I'll let you girls hang out. I'm going to give this secret message to your mom...I heard it's something about Christmas surprises!" she told the girls.

The girls squealed with excitement as Nurse Kali handed me a small slip of green and red paper that listed the Christmas activities going on in the hospital. There were quite a few: Slime making with Child Life, gingerbread house and cookie decorating in the activity room, gifts delivered from Santa's elves, and a hot chocolate bar for parents in the family lounge. At the bottom, it said: "Any of these activities can be brought to your child's room if necessary".

Looking up, I smiled. "Would it be ok if Child Life came to Ari's room while Ari's receiving her infusion? We may venture out of the room a little later."

"For sure! Not a problem at all! I will let them know, and they should be around shortly!"

She turned and walked out of the door.

Emilia jumped up and down. "I'm so excited!" she exclaimed, and she ran over to the window to watch millions of snowflakes fall and blanket the ground in a cold embrace.

I looked over at Ari and watched as the chemotherapy trickled into her body. She was frowning. I hated this life for her. I wished more than anything that she was healthy and able to live a normal three-year-old life. *What kind of life is it to sit in a hospital bed on Christmas day and have poison pumped into you? Not a very fair one. Not a very friendly one at all.*

"Muma?"

"What is it, Ari?"

"Do you think Zola is here today?" she asked.

"Maybe, honey. When we go out a little later, we might see her," I said.

She smiled a hopeful smile.

Zola is Ari's favorite person to see at the hospital. The week of Ari's diagnosis and first cycle of treatment, her hospital room had been the one right next to Zola's room. I had seen Zola through her window as we were brought up to Ari's room from the ER, but it wasn't until later that week that Ari met her. Zola had been in the hallway, riding one of the hospital's tricycles, and she had paused in the doorway, waving at Ari. Ari's face had immediately lit up, and she had waved back. From then on, Ari and Zola have become treatment buddies and have spent a lot of time together while in the hospital.

Zola was also recently diagnosed and is only two months further into treatment than Ari is. She is battling Stage 4 Rhabdomyosarcoma, which is an aggressive childhood cancer that starts in the muscle tissue. She is three years old, just like Ari, and is very sweet and intelligent. I have talked to Zola's parents for many hours about everything cancer and life related, so it has been really nice for both me and Ari to have that relatable type of support.

Just then, there was a knock on the door. Two festive-looking Child Life specialists walked in with slime and mix-ins in their hands and smiles on their faces.

"Merry Christmas, girls! Does anyone here like to make slime?"

Emilia ran over from the window.

"Me! Me! Me!" she shouted.

Ari nodded, her lips curving into a shy smile.

"Awesome! We have some slime already made for you, so you can make it red or green and add some fun little Christmas mix-ins to make it festive!"

As the girls excitedly got to work, I looked at the Christmas activities list Nurse Kali gave me.

* * *

I walked over to the table with a snowflake tablecloth. There was a crockpot of hot chocolate and bowls of marshmallows, crushed candy canes, and some cool whip. I shuffled down the table as I poured a cup of hot chocolate and topped it with two spoonfuls of marshmallows, a heaping spoonful of cool whip, and a pinch of crushed candy cane. At the very end of the table, a lady handed me a 25 dollar Visa gift card and said "'Merry Christmas! Please enjoy this gift from our Triple C staff!'".

As I walked away, I smiled at their generosity and raised the cup of hot chocolate to my lips. I brought it back down quickly and licked my lips; it was still burning hot. I looked around the room while I waited. Then, on the other side of the room, I saw a young black couple: Zola's parents. They were picking out some festively decorated Christmas cookies.

I walked over to them.

"Hi Valarie! Hi Trevor!"

"Hey Norah! How are you, dear? And how is little Ari doing?"

"We're all hanging in there, I guess. First day of cycle four."

"Third day of cycle 12 for Zola. This round has really knocked her out; she's been sleeping for most of the past two days."

"Aww, poor baby. I hate to hear that."

"I know, we hate it for her. Well, I'm sure Zola will want to see Ari when she feels up to it, so we might stop by Ari's room later today or tomorrow, if that's ok."

"Yes, Ari would love that, I'm sure. Well, Merry Christmas! I'm sorry we all have to spend it the cancer way, though."

"Yeah, us too. But thanks, Merry Christmas to you too!"

Before turning to head back to Ari's room, I grabbed three Christmas tree cookies from one of the tables. Ari's weight struggled to stay stable during treatment weeks, and lately, sweets were one of the few things Ari had an appetite for, so I was going to make sure she got in some yummy calories by mouth in addition to her tube feedings.

When I returned to Ari's room, they had finished making slime and were now decorating a gingerbread house. Nurse Kali was just finishing taking Ari's vitals. Emilia was working intently on perfecting the sugary house, but Ari's eyelids kept drooping, and she held a blue vomit bag close to her chest.

I walked over to her and kissed the top of her head; no curls touched my lips.

"Aww, honey, are you not feeling very well?"

"No," she sleepily replied.

Why? Why does this have to be her life? She should be playing in the snow right now—not sitting in a hospital bed feeling miserable. I wanted to scream or cry or fall to the floor and curl up in a ball. But I chose to do nothing; I remained calm and composed. Because in the end, none of those actions could change anything about the situation at all.

"Finished!" Emilia exclaimed as she placed the last gumdrop on the roof of the house.

"Wow! Wonderful job, honey!" I said, mustering a smile.

Arielle smiled slightly as she observed the finished gingerbread house. Then, I noticed a children's book of the story of Hansel and Gretel sitting next to her. *Child Life must have given that to her with the gingerbread house kit.*

The cruel irony in the story haunted me as I flipped through the pages. Just like the gingerbread house in the story, Ari's body was so very sweet on the outside but overwhelmed by the danger that lurked within.

TO CELEBRATE WHAT KILLS (ONE WEEK LATER)

Home, sweet home I thought as we walked through the door. It had been a long six days at the hospital. We ended up having to stay one night longer than anticipated because Ari's oxygen levels had been a bit lower than the doctors would have liked during our "supposed-to-be" last night there. Her nausea was also very persistent despite medication, so the team wanted her to stay until they felt more safe about her going home. It was just precautionary, really. Because the worst thing would be for us to get home and then have to turn right back around because things had gotten worse instead of better.

Luckily, Ari felt somewhat better today, and her oxygen levels had stayed stable overnight, so we were allowed to come home for three weeks so Ari could rest and recover before cycle five on January 24th.

It was already New Year's Eve, and we still had the rest of Christmas to celebrate. I glanced at all of the unopened gifts under the Christmas tree and then at Ari in my arms. We may have to wait another few days. She was still feeling pretty miserable, I could tell. But I was glad we were finally home, so we could celebrate the holidays properly. Ari was officially halfway through phase one, so a celebration definitely felt needed.

* * *

The girls had gone to bed. They were exhausted after six broken nights of sleep in the hospital. I was, too, but Ivaan and I had always celebrated New Year's Eve together since freshman year of college, and I wasn't going to let cancer break our tradition.

We sat on the soft, grey sofa in the living room. The room was dark aside from the bright glow of the television that illuminated our faces. Two glasses of sparkling champagne sat on the coffee table in front of us.

The New Year's Eve program sounded through the television. I watched sleepily, determined to stay awake for one more hour. I leaned against the arm of the couch on a pillow, with my legs crossed. Ivaan slumped back, his knees jutting out further than his feet.

I looked at him, searching for the man I had fallen in love with twelve years ago. *What is going through his mind? He never tells me anything anymore.*

"I love you, honey," I said. "Are you ok?"

"Yeah, I'm fine. I think Ari's diagnosis has just been a bit distracting and overwhelming, that's all," he said, looking down.

I hated the physical and emotional distance cancer had created between us. It was as if we hardly knew each other anymore. We rarely touched each other. Ivaan was rarely home anymore. He was always working, and then some nights when he comes home late, he smells faintly of alcohol. I knew he had to be drinking again. He had been a heavy drinker in college—partying any chance he got—which I had never liked, so he had changed his habits for me. I was trying so hard to not be upset with him, though. *I know we all cope in our own ways, but I just wish he would talk to me about what was going on in his head.* The silence was deafening sometimes. I could hardly stand it.

But maybe I was coping in the wrong ways as well. I had let my anxiety become nearly uncontrollable, and my mind never stopped racing. I was barely sleeping, barely eating, barely breathing.

Ivaan and I were living our own separate lives. Messy lives that seemed confined to our own bodies and minds but were fully on display. Quite simply, cancer had fractured us—both as a couple and as the individuals we used to be.

Wasn't I the one who told Emilia to lean on God? Why was it so hard for me to listen to my own advice? I wasn't sure, but I knew I had to start. I didn't want "fractured" to become "broken".

My eyes glanced at the television. There were only 30 more minutes until the ball dropped. I looked back at the slack expression on Ivaan's face and then back at the New Year's program on the television. I took a strangled breath in, half rolling my eyes as tears of frustration threatened to reveal my inner turmoil. *How much longer can I sit here?* The stale air between us was becoming painfully stifling. All of the sudden, I didn't feel like celebrating. I stood abruptly to my feet, said night to Ivaan, and walked to my room to lay in bed.

What was even the point? Celebrating New Year's meant celebrating time. Time passing. Time lost. Time ticking. The one thing that is killing my little girl just as quickly as the cancer festering inside of her tiny body.

CHAPTER 17

CRINKLED CONFETTI (TWO WEEKS LATER)

Emilia walked down the stairs rubbing her eyes. Ivaan, Ari, and I were standing around the kitchen island with party hats on. Em's eyes lit up as soon as she saw the unicorn birthday cake in front of us.

"Happy Birthday, Em!" Ari shouted.

"Happy Eighth Birthday, sweetie!" Ivaan and I quickly added.

"Yay! Thank you!" Em giggled and jumped up and down.

"Daddy said we can have cake for breakfast!" Ari exclaimed.

Em's eyes widened momentarily, but I interjected.

"Well, I didn't quite agree with that," I said, shooting Ivaan a look.

"Mum, come on...please! It's my birthday! Can't you just pretend I'm Ari for one day?"

"Em, you can have it with some breakfast, but I'm not letting you or Ari fill up on sugar this early. Ari has a sensitive stomach right now."

"But I don't!" Em complained.

"That doesn't matter, ok?" I snapped.

"Ugh, it's always about Ari! Even on *my* birthday!"

"Emilia, honey, you know that's not fair," Ivaan tried.

"But it's true," Em retorted.

I stood, silent. I had never seen Emilia behave like this before. *Was I really directing too much attention towards Ari? But how could I not? She has cancer.*

All of a sudden, I lost it. Completely. I couldn't stop crying. This life was way too hard and confusing. If anything wasn't fair, it was that cancer had somehow made our perfectly happy life a living hell.

"Fine! Eat the cake! I don't care anymore! I'm going to go lay down," I yelled before storming out of the kitchen.

As I left, I heard Emilia start to cry and say, "I didn't mean to make Mum upset. Now she really hates me, doesn't she?" Ivaan started to respond, but I was already too far to hear what he had to say. The last thought I had before falling asleep traveled to my heart, and I believed it: *cancer has made me a terrible mother.*

* * *

I walked up to Emilia's room and found her writing at her desk. I knocked lightly on her wall. She turned to look at me.

"Hey, Em. Can I come in?"

"Sure."

"What are you up to? I asked gently.

"Just writing you a sorry letter," she said, frowning.

"Oh," I said, surprised. "Well actually, Em, I was coming up here to say sorry to you."

"But why? I was the mean one."

"No, honey, I was wrong. I'm sorry for yelling. And I'm sorry I've been focusing so much on Ari lately. It's just that she's really sick, Em, and I'm so scared. But I never wanted to make you feel left out or unloved. Not ever. I'm so sorry, honey. Will you forgive me?"

Her eyes were wide and sad.

"I forgive you," she said as she stretched out her arms and cautiously hugged me and my five-month baby bump. "Dad said you have a lot to worry about and that having a baby in your belly makes you extra stressed sometimes. So I'm sorry I gave you a hard time about everything this morning."

She paused, looking up at me.

"Thanks, honey. I guess Dad's right. So many big changes happened at the same time. It's been hard for all of us to process. But I'm trying, Em."

"I know. I'm scared too, Mum," she said. "I don't understand why Ari had to get sick. She doesn't deserve it."

"You're right, honey. Ari doesn't deserve to be sick. It's not fair. It's not fair that children get cancer. It's not fair that anyone does." I paused, waiting for the right words to enter my mind, but none came. "I'm sorry, honey, I don't know what else to say."

"It's ok, Mum. You don't have to know everything. Some things just don't make sense. But it's not your fault, Mum—none of this is."

I smiled.

"Thanks, honey. I needed to hear that," I said and kissed the top of her head. Embracing her slender frame in my arms, I hugged her warmly. *I hope she knows how much I love her.* I squeezed her tighter.

I pulled away, smiling.

"What?" Emilia asked, giggling.

"I'm sorry today had a rough start, honey. To make it up to you, how about we go out for ice cream before dinner and before dad gets home."

Her eyes lit up.

"Really!? You're the best!"

* * *

The ice cream scooper bulldozed through the softly frozen surface. Leaving a melty trail behind, it rolled hunks of yellow cake and rainbow sprinkles into a creamy vanilla scoop the size of a baseball.

The scooper, a young lady with bronze skin, plopped the scoop into a cup and topped it with a heap of whipped cream, sprinkles, and a cherry. Then, she proceeded to scoop a ball of fruity red, yellow, and blue, plopped it into a cup, and impaled it with a toothpick that had a superhero-shaped marshmallow stuck at the top.

She stepped over to the cash register.

"Alright, your total comes to nine dollars and seventy-two cents."

I started to dig out my credit card from my wallet, struggling a bit with Ari in my arms.

Then, an older gentleman approached us from the left with a ten dollar bill in his hand.

"Here Miss," he said, shakily holding out the money. "Please allow me to pay."

His eyes were kind.

I stared for a moment, failing to process his offer.

"Oh!" I finally said. "Are you sure?"

He nodded.

"How kind! Thank you very much, Sir!"

"My pleasure!" He winked. "I miss being able to buy my son ice cream, so really, this feels like an honor. My son is probably smiling down at us right now. He never missed a chance to make a fellow warrior smile, and as long as I live, that will remain true," he said, looking up. His eyes glittered with tears.

My hand rose to my heart at his sentiment.

"That is so sweet. I'm sure your son is very proud of you," I said, smiling sympathetically.

He smiled and gave a slow nod. Before walking away, he offered Ari a gentle fist bump.

I turned, watching him hobble away with his cane. I smiled and looked at Em and Ari.

"Well, that was very kind of him, wasn't it?" I exclaimed.

"Yeah. He was a nice old man," Em agreed.

Ari smiled sweetly and nodded.

* * *

It was a little after 7 o'clock at night. I had noodles boiling in a pot on the stove. Em had requested mac n' cheese and grilled chicken for her birthday dinner. I was depending on Ivaan to get the new grill up and running, but he still wasn't home from work.

At least that's where he said he was two hours ago.

Suddenly, the door creaked open. Emilia stopped mixing the fruit salad and she ran towards the door.

"Dad's home!" she shouted.

My head turned towards the door, and I saw Ivaan standing in the doorway, his face emotionless and his eyes spacey.

I rushed over.

"Yep, Dad's home," I said dryly. "How about you continue mixing that fruit salad, ok, Em?"

"Ok!" she agreed, skipping away.

I waited until she was back in the kitchen. I looked Ivaan up and down and pressed closer to him momentarily.

"Ivaan, you smell like alcohol," I said under my breath.

His eyes widened, and he froze.

"What?" I snapped. "You think I haven't noticed? You come home late almost every night, you barely touch me, let alone look at me, you..." I paused, thinking. "You aren't the man I fell in love with, Ivaan. It's like I don't even know you anymore."

Tears collected in my eyes. Ivaan stood staring, his face slack.

"And of all nights. Really? Did you really think that would go well for you? It's our daughter's birthday, Ivaan. What were you thinking?"

The tears were falling now, streaming down my face like rain on a window.

"Ivaan, I mean, you have a daughter who's fighting for her life with stage four cancer, a wife who's up to her chin with stress and carrying your son in her uterus, and another daughter who's trying to adjust to all of this, and right now, is depending on you to make her favorite dinner for her birthday. And you're out drinking? Seriously? I suggest you get your shit together."

"Nor, I..."

"Ivaan, please. I don't have the energy. Don't make me listen to another one of your bullshit excuses. You're walking on a real thin line, ok? Why can't you see that?"

I sniffled. My throat felt painfully tight. I knew only one thing would fix it. I turned and ran into our room, closing the door. I started to let everything out: all of the frustration, hurt, grief, anger. I sobbed loudly into the darkness.

"Muma? What's wrong?"

I froze. Ari was in here. Her precious ears had heard my ugly anguish. Sniffling, I wiped my face quickly.

"Nothing, honey. What are you doing here in the dark all by yourself?" I asked, concerned.

"I don't feel good."

My heart shrank in my chest. With my eyes finally adjusted to the dark, I reached out to feel her forehead. She was very warm. We would have to go to the emergency department as a routine precaution in case her port was infected.

"Oh, honey. I'm going to have to take you to the hospital."

She started whining.

"I know, honey. I'm sorry," I said, scooping her up in my arms.

I walked out into the kitchen. Ivaan was sitting at the table, and Emilia was mixing the fruit dip for the salad. *I hated what I had to do. Emilia would be absolutely crushed.*

"I'm going to have to take Ari to the hospital. She's running a fever," I said quickly as if it would make it less painful to hear.

Emilia's smile was immediately replaced with a frown.

"Nooo!" she cried.

"I know, honey. I'm so sorry," I said. "I really hate to do this."

"It's ok, honey," Ivaan said. "We can have a daddy-daughter date."

She stopped crying, but a frown was still painted on her face.

"I'm going to call Aunt Indie to come over; she can watch the *both* of you," I said, my eyes burning into Ivaan's.

I turned my gaze to Emilia. "Please, Em, try to have fun, ok? I know this whole day hasn't gone how you planned, and I'm sorry, but I'll make it up to you once Ari and I are home, ok?"

Still frowning, she nodded.

Moments later, Indie knocked on the door, and then I was off to CCH with Ari whimpering in the backseat.

I hate this. So much. This shouldn't have to be her life.

And even though it was Emilia's birthday, my mind couldn't help but wonder if cancer would allow Ari to turn four years old in three months.

RECOVERING RED (TWO WEEKS LATER)

One at a time, I gripped Ari's bruised, atrophied calves in my hand while I pushed on her purple light up shoes. I turned to Em and Indie standing behind me.

"Ok, Em. We'll be back soon. Be good for Aunt Indie."

"Ok. Love you Mum."

"Love you too, honey."

Ari blew both of them a kiss as I picked her up to carry her to the car. I walked outside to see Ivaan in the driver's seat with the car started. The window was rolled down, the radio's music audible. His arm was hanging out, and he was tapping his fingers against the car to the beat of the music.

"Ivaan," I said sternly, "you know I need the car to take Ari to the hospital to get her blood drawn."

He lifted his sunglasses up.

"Nor, I remember," he said, slightly hurt. "Hop in."

"Oh, ok. You're coming? I thought you were going out with work friends?"

"Yeah, I was. But I told Brian I couldn't make it anymore." He paused, smiling softly. "This is more important."

I touched his shoulder, staring into his electric green eyes.

"Thank you," I whispered.

"No, thank you," he said. "For showing me what a foolish ass I was being."

I laughed at his word choice.

"No, really," he said. "I'm sorry."

"It's ok. You're here now. That's all that matters. Let's not live in the past," I said, looking at Ari in the backseat. "We can't afford that."

He smiled gratefully, and smoothed his hand up my thigh, pushing my skirt up just slightly.

Just that little bit of friction had rekindled a spark between us. It wasn't strong, but at least it was present.

I smiled bashfully as we backed out of the driveway, his hand still on my upper thigh.

* * *

Ivaan held Ari close in his muscular arms, trying to comfort her while the nurse accessed the port in her chest. Ari whimpered only slightly.

The nurse collected several tubes of blood and flushed Ari's port with normal saline to clear the line.

"Good job, sweetie," she congratulated. She had a Russian accent. She turned to us. "You are free to go anywhere in hospital; we call back in one hour with results."

"Ok, thank you." Ivaan said.

He pulled down Ari's shirt over the tubing from her port and stood up with her in his arms. He placed Ari into her wheelchair, and started to wheel her out of the room. I followed.

"How about we grab a snack. Does that sound good?" Ivaan asked.

"Yeah," I said. "That sounds nice."

We went down to the second floor and stopped at the hospital's cafeteria. Ivaan grabbed a quinoa protein bowl, I grabbed a coffee, and Ari requested some frosted animal crackers and apple juice. After paying, we sat down at a circular table by a window.

I reached behind Ari's wheelchair, unzipped her feeding tube backpack, and pressed "Run" on her feeding tube pump to start her on her daily feed, which would continue for the next 18 hours. At this point in treatment, she could only manage to consume a quarter or less of the nutrition her body needed, so this would be the routine until she could eat enough by mouth to sustain her body's needs. I assumed it would be awhile, though, since her treatment and symptoms are intense, and fighting cancer burns an insane amount of calories.

"Wow, this is delicious!" Ivaan exclaimed, shoveling some quinoa and veggies into his mouth. "Want to try some, Nor? You should have something other than coffee."

"Yeah, ok," I said, pleasantly surprised by his thoughtfulness.

He carefully filled the spoon with the nutritious contents of the bowl—making sure to include a little bit of everything in one bite. Holding his hand under the spoon, he raised it up to my open mouth. I closed my lips around the spoon as he slid it backwards, towards him. *He's right. This is good.*

A thin layer of avocado dressing coated my lips. Ivaan took a napkin, folded it into a triangle, and wiped my lips delicately.

I giggled.

"Thanks, hon," I said. "It's very good."

"Please, have some more."

He smiled, staring lovingly into my eyes. I stared back for the longest time. His handsome green eyes were mesmerizing.

The crinkle of Ari's animal cookie bag brought me back. I pulled away slowly, still smiling, and I took hold of the spoon in his hand.

As I spooned a bite into my mouth, I glanced at Ari. She sat slowly munching on a pink frosted animal cookie. Her head was directed to her right. All of the people in the room seemed to entertain her young mind. But they were just depressing to me. They were doing the same thing as us: sitting, waiting, hoping, doubting. Everyone in this room had a painful reason for being here.

* * *

Ari sat in an infusion clinic chair with a white blanket wrapped around her little body up to her neck. An IV bag filled with O negative blood dripped into the tubing that led to Ari's port and into her body. Her results had come back very low. No wonder she had so many bruises and was so pale. Her platelets, hemoglobin, and white blood cells all met transfusion levels, so it would be another three hours before we got home. Since she didn't make counts, she would not be able to start chemo tomorrow. We would have to wait another week to recheck and reassess. The nurse said it was likely due to the combination of the last treatment cycle and the viral infection Ari got that landed us on the oncology floor for two days about a week and a half ago.

This isn't the first time this has happened throughout Ari's treatment journey so far, but every time it does happen, it makes me just as worried. I hated that not meeting counts meant delaying treatment. Yes, waiting one week for her counts to recover meant one week longer of rest with no hospital or chemo, but no chemo means nothing is helping to kill the cancer. And even though count recovery is a common mild setback for oncology patients, it couldn't help the sinister fact that an extra week of no chemo—no poison filtering into her body—meant a week of the cancerous cells being able to do as they please just a little more easily.

HEARTS OF GOLD (THREE WEEKS LATER)

I gripped the pole of Ari's IV stand, wheeling it cautiously behind her. She was on one of the hospital's tricycles, so I made sure to follow at a steady pace. If I walked too quickly, the tubing could get wrapped up under a wheel; if I followed too slowly, the tubing could stretch too far and pull at the point of insert in her port. Either way, if I messed up, it would cause her more pain. I definitely didn't want that.

Zola rode next to Ari. Their bald heads glowed from the gleam of the fluorescent lights on the ceiling. Their mint green hospital gowns clothed their small bodies loosely. Their boney knees peaked out from under their gowns as they peddled. And their small, high-pitched giggles echoed throughout the empty hallways.

Although I hated the circumstances that had led them to meet each other, I loved the sister-like bond they had formed. Because of their common battles, they connected with one another in ways only they could understand. An awfully dreadful disease had formed an unbreakable friendship.

Along with Zola and her mum, Ari and I were going to check out what special activities were going on in the craft center. It was Valentine's Day across the world, but it was "Golden Hearts Day" on the oncology floor at Cardinal Children's Hospital. Instead of screaming red and pink, every warrior and their family were screaming gold—the awareness color for childhood cancer. The hallway walls of Triple C were decorated with many golden hearts for the occasion. Triple C staff tried their best to make having fun possible for their young patients. In the medical world, the only thing more healing than medicine and rest is smiling and laughter.

I had promised Ari she could spend the whole day having fun with Zola. Zola would be discharged later today. And on her way out, she would be ringing the bell to signify her completion of pre-surgery chemotherapy. The final bit of her last dose was trickling into her body as we walked. Her post-chemo scans would be a week from now. I was so happy for Zola and her sweet family. Ringing the bell is such a huge accomplishment in the oncology world. It symbolizes hope and victory. And it's a shame that not every patient gets the chance to hear the bell ring from their own hands.

I pray Ari will get that chance in two months, but for today, we will celebrate Zola.

"Muma!" Ari shouted.

I froze, worried I had kinked her IV line by accident. I frantically searched the trailing tubing and realized I had not. *Thank goodness.*

I looked up to see Woody, Triple C's therapy dog, and his handler, a young nerdy-looking guy named Gus.

The girls reached out and patted Woody's freshly-groomed, fluffy golden fur. He looked especially handsome today with a heart-patterned bandana around his neck. The girls loved him. Everyone did. His calmness and loving personality was instantly emotionally healing.

"How's it going, girls?" Gus inquired. "Woody is so excited to see you both! He's been talking about you all morning!"

They giggled in response—so did Valerie and I.

* * *

Zola and Ari sat nestled together in Ari's hospital bed; they were intently watching Tangled. Ari was receiving the rest of her chemo infusion for the day, and in only 15 minutes, Zola would get to walk down the Warrior Path to ring the bell. Because of that, the atmosphere of the room was much cheerier than usual.

I turned my gaze to Valerie as she started to speak.

"I can't believe Zola's already at this point. It's so surreal."

"Zola's definitely a tough cookie," I said, looking over at Zola in Ari's bed. "And you are too, Val," I said, laying my hand on her forearm and smiling.

She looked at me with glittering eyes.

"Aww, thanks Nor! You and Ari are tough as well, and she's going to make it to this point, too. I'm sure of it."

"Thanks, Val. I hope so. I wish I had your certainty."

She chuckled.

"Oh, you do, girl. It's called faith. It's in there; you just gotta pause and remember sometimes."

I smiled. And at that, Ari's nurse came in. She unhooked her from her chemo for the night and replaced her empty nutrition and anti-nausea bags with full ones.

"Good job, kiddo," she said as she wrapped a blood pressure cuff around Ari's thin arm. Then she turned to Zola. "So Zola, I heard you have a Chemo Clap Out in a few minutes! That's exciting!"

"I'm so happy!" Zola exclaimed.

"You should be! I'm happy for you, too!" Nurse Tessa added.

She pressed a button on the heart monitor and typed Ari's vitals into the computer. Then she looked up.

"Alright," she said, "I think it's time! Would you like to head to the Warrior Path, Zola?"

Zola sat up promptly and jumped off of the bed.

"Come on, Mum! Let's go!" she shouted excitedly, extending her arm.

Valerie took hold of Zola's small hand in hers.

"We'll see you there!" Valerie said to Ari and me.

With a wave, they headed out the door.

Nurse Tessa helped Ari into her wheelchair and wheeled her IV pole closer. Then, we headed out the door and down the hallway. We parked Ari near the end of the Warrior Path—near the bell and elevator—so that she would be able to say goodbye to Zola after she rang the bell.

Many doctors, nurses, parents, and children of all ages and at various places in their cancer treatments lined the hallway leading to the elevator.

The applause and congratulation began to sound at the other end of the hallway. I watched as Zola and Valerie made their way down the Warrior Path. Zola—in a gold, sparkly tutu and a princess crown—skipped next to her mother with a sweet smile on her face. Valerie held Zola's hand in her right hand and wiped tears from her eyes with her left hand.

Gold confetti flew up in the air from nurses' hands and fluttered down onto the floor. Some of it, however, managed to get stuck in Valerie's fluffy black hair. She laughed, trying to brush some of it away with her hand as she walked.

Zola and Valerie neared the end and headed towards the bell hanging on the wall. Zola slowly stepped up onto the tiny step stool. She stared at the bell in front of her for a second and then at the small crowd anxiously awaiting her next action. Valerie whispered something quietly to Zola, and then Zola reached up and grasped the rope in her hands. She shook it timidly at first, the metal on the rope barely grazing the inside of the bell. Then, she pulled the rope back and forth with sureness and strength, and the ringing of hope and courage sounded. The crowd clapped for her accomplishment, and Zola turned to face us, smiling proudly.

Then, she leapt off of the stool and ran over to Ari and me.

Valerie followed. She reached out and hugged me. We stood for a moment, just taking in each other's comfort and presence.

Zola went to the side of Ari's wheelchair, reaching out to hug her. Ari wrapped her arms around Zola. They pulled away, and Ari presented a small teddy bear to Zola as a present. Zola smiled and squealed with delight.

So very precious. A tear rolled down my cheek.

Valerie and Zola stepped into the elevator, pressing a button. Valerie's mascara was smeared, but her radiant, white-teethed smile confirmed the tears were happy ones. Zola's sweet smile and innocent wave made my heart melt. The large metal doors closed slowly, eating away at the final image of Zola and her mum until it was gone completely.

More tears rolled down my cheeks and Ari seemed a bit melancholy as well. It wasn't a forever goodbye, but it would be a little while before we saw them again.

The atmosphere felt odd. There was mainly excitement and joy, but a heavy touch of loneliness and sadness hung in the air. Maybe it was because celebrating one patient's victory didn't ensure everyone else would one day, too, have one to celebrate. Or maybe it was because the unknown was haunting, and victory was really just a loosely-defined word because cancer could so quickly and easily change it to heartbreak.

I didn't know for sure, but I knew what was influencing the atmosphere the most: love.

KYRA FAITH

What a short word for such a powerful emotion. A force that touches every inch of the body yet is somehow difficult to express in words. With the ability to love, comes the inevitably of sadness and heartbreak. Just like a peak and a valley, neither one can exist without the other.

CHAPTER 20

ALIVE (TWO WEEKS LATER)

The sliding glass door let out a drawn-out squeak as I pushed it closed behind me. The house was quiet. Aunt Indie had taken Arielle and Emilia to the movie theater. It's the first time Ivaan and I had the house to ourselves since before Ari's diagnosis. I had gone outside to read since Ivaan had wanted to take a shower, but it had been an hour or longer, so I wanted to see what he was up to now.

I waddled down the hallway, my hand over my seventh-month baby bump.

A wide section of the wood floor in the hallway glowed from light streaming out of the soon-to-be baby's room. I peaked in, leaning on the frame of the doorway. Ivaan held a paint roller in his hand with a tub of paint at his feet. A baby crib stood partly assembled in the middle of the room.

I smiled. *His sober behavior has definitely been refreshing; I'm glad I was finally able to get through to him. Busying himself with getting ready for the new baby is definitely a better way for him to cope.*

His upper-arm muscles flexed as he coated the wall in a soft pastel green. We had decided on a friendly dinosaur theme for the nursery. For some reason, it just seemed right. *Our baby boy would come into this world with strength and resilience.*

I shifted my weight, a floorboard creaking beneath me.

"Looks nice, honey," I said softly.

Ivaan stopped and turned in my direction. His vibrant green eyes revitalized my heart, making it beat faster. He smiled dashingly.

"Thanks, Nor," he said, looking around and slowly walking towards me. "All of this is definitely making me really excited for this little guy."

He gently placed his hands on my belly, and smiled down at me. His handsome green eyes mesmerized me. I stared into them, and he stared back into mine. I smoothed my hands up his hands and wrists and grasped his forearms, feeling his muscular build.

He slowly leaned in closer to me, his waist pressing up against my belly. His face inched closer and closer to mine until I could feel the warmth of his breath. Our lips pressed together—tenderly at first and then with passionate force.

I pivoted, pushing him against the wall, my hands on his shoulders. His hands slid down my frame, resting on my hips. We paused for a moment, just staring into each other's eyes and breathing heavily. Sparks turned into flames. The fire between us was back. I felt alive. I smiled with triumph, utmost gratitude filling my heart. *Cancer couldn't break us after all.*

He leaned down again, his lips against mine. He stepped forward and I backward. As our bodies moved toward nothing in particular, our hands moved with purpose. I smoothed my hands over his back, perspiration licking my palms. His hands traveled down my spine, resting at my lower back.

His hands reached out behind me, tagging the wall with heavy impact. My back collided with the wall as well, and I titled my head back as Ivaan moved his lips down my neck and onto my chest.

Suddenly, the coolness of the wall against the bareness of my back became oddly unsettling. I lifted my left hand up to my eyes. Its peachy, pink color was covered in a pale green undertone.

I started laughing.

"Ivaan, honey, stop," I said softly, still laughing.

The warmness of his lips left my neck. And he stared into my eyes, confused.

"What is it?" he asked.

I turned my left hand for him to see. A smirk replaced the confusion on his face. He peeled his hands from the wall. They, too, were painted a pale green.

He looked down at his right foot, and I followed his gaze. His foot rested in a shallow pool of soft pastel green paint; he had stepped right in the middle of the paint tub.

He let out a chuckle as he breathed out, shaking his head. I giggled.

"Oh, honey," I said, resting my hand on his chest and laughing into it before looking back up.

Along with his smirk, confusion had returned to his face.

"That's weird. I barely even noticed," he said. "It's as if the world around us had disappeared for just a moment. Only you and I existed."

I smiled, staring into his dreamy eyes.

"Ignorance is bliss," I said, kissing him once more. "Too bad the world wouldn't let us keep it."

CHAPTER 21

SCANNING THE FUTURE (THREE WEEKS LATER)

Only two days ago, Ari had completed her final round of chemotherapy for phase one of treatment for stage 4 high risk neuroblastoma. And just like Zola, she had walked down Warrior Path and rang the bell. Ari, Emilia, Ivaan, and I had been overjoyed that day. We had celebrated all day, doing anything Ari and Emilia had pleased. We had even all gone outside when it got dark to catch fireflies and watch the starry sky. It had been a magical day. It had felt like the battle was over.

But, as I sat with Ari on my lap in the radiology waiting room, I knew the journey was far from over. She had survived six intensive rounds of chemotherapy, four full body MIBG scans, more nights in the hospital than I could count, many blood transfusions, and countless pokes since the day of her diagnosis just six months ago, yet that wasn't enough. Not for cancer. Cancer demanded more suffering. I hated that with everything inside of me. It wasn't fair—none of this was.

I gripped Ivaan's warm hand. He sat in the chair next to me. The waiting room was quiet—tensely so. I breathed in and out deeply, trying to calm my mind, and I prayed to God that Ari's post-chemo scans would look encouraging. If they did, the doctors would proceed with the last step of phase one: surgery to remove the tumor above her left kidney. But if they weren't, I suppose they would do more rounds of chemo or something else—or nothing else. *Gosh, I don't want to have to find that out. God, please don't let me have to find that out. Please allow Ari's scans to be improved from three weeks ago.*

"Arielle," a male nurse with long, wavy brown hair called out.

I stood up with Ari in my hands, and Ivaan took her into his, cradling her like a baby. I grabbed my purse and followed Ivaan to where the nurse was standing. He smiled and led us into the painfully familiar world of radiology that hid behind the double doors.

* * *

Arielle's eyes flickered open. She had finally come off of the anesthesia.

"Hey, baby girl," Ivaan said softly.

I took hold of her unicorn stuffed animal by her side and placed it under her arms. She grasped her little hand around my pointer and middle finger before letting go and hugging the unicorn close to her chest.

"Hi, sweetie," I said.

She smiled slightly before closing her eyes once more.

A nurse knocked on the wall before parting open the curtains. She came in, holding a plastic cup in her hands. I had asked for some apple juice for Ari for when she was up and ready to try to drink something.

"Thank you," I said, taking it from her hands.

"No problem," she replied.

She walked over to Ari's bedside, her brown curls bouncing behind her. She reached up and lightly pulsated the IV bag of fluids hanging on the IV pole to the left of Ari's bed. Then she typed something into the computer.

At the sound of the clicking keys, Ari opened her eyes and turned her head towards the nurse. The nurse directed her gaze on Ari and stepped forward, lightly touching Ari's shoulder.

"How are you doing, Ari?" she asked calmly.

Ari breathed in deeply, stretching her arms above her head.

"Sleepy," she said softly and slowly.

The nurse chuckled softly.

"Oh yeah? Did you have a good nap?"

"Emm-hmm," Ari replied, still only partly present.

"That's good. Well, once you feel ready to sit up, we'll get you all set to go back home so you can rest, ok?"

Ari nodded.

Smiling, the nurse walked out of the partly curtained cubicle.

"Look what the nurse left for you, honey," I said a few minutes later. I held up the cup of apple juice so she could see.

Expressionless, she sat up slowly and reached out her arms towards the cup in my hands.

"Good job, honey. Here you go," I said, holding the straw up to her mouth.

She closed her chapped lips around the skinny plastic tube and took three small sips before pulling away to lick her lips.

"Is it yummy, honey?" Ivaan asked.

Ari nodded slowly, smiling.

The nurse knocked and parted the curtains.

"It's me again!" she said as she entered. She turned her gaze to Ari. "I'm so glad to see you sitting up so quickly! Are you ready to get home?" she asked in a very enthusiastic voice.

Ari nodded.

"Good! Well, all I have to do before you leave is deaccess your port, so if you want to hold mom or dad's hand or anything, you can do that now, ok?"

Ivaan walked over and held Ari's hands in his.

Ari started to breathe quickly, but she stayed still and calm for the nurse. The nurse peeled off the dressing and wiped the area around her port with an antiseptic wipe to get rid of any bacteria. After discarding the wipe, she took a syringe of normal saline and flushed it through her port to clear the line, followed by a syringe of heparin to prevent infection and keep blood from clotting. Taking the needle in her fingertips, she pulled it out at a 90 degree angle until a click sounded. Ari flinched just slightly. The nurse dropped the needle into the sharps container mounted on the wall to her right before cleaning Ari's port once again and applying pressure to the site with gauze. After a few seconds, she unpeeled a bandaid and placed it over the gauze to hold it in place.

"Great job, brave girl! You did awesome today!"

Ari smiled and pointed at something beyond the curtains in front of her. I looked and so did the nurse. It was the sticker station—Ari's favorite.

Understanding, the nurse laughed.

"Of course you can have a sticker, Ari. In fact, you were so brave today that I think you can have two or three! Why don't you get changed out of your gown and then you guys are free to go," she said, handing me the discharge papers.

We nodded with understanding and thanked her. With a wave, she left, so Ari could get changed.

I pulled out an outfit from my purse. Ivaan pulled Ari's gown over her head and helped me thread her arms and legs through her outfit. *We made an efficient team.* Ari had transformed from a hospital kid to her regular self in the matter of two minutes. *I could only pray that this scan's results would allow her life to follow the same pattern.*

Ivaan picked Ari up, setting her down in her small, pink wheelchair. He wheeled her over to the sticker station, so she could pick out a few stickers.

I followed, feeling every cell in my body become instantly contaminated with anxiety as I took in the seemingly endless row of curtained bays that other sick children were in. *This world is so cruel. Every little thing seems to trigger me after Ari's diagnosis. I feel like a skeleton of who I used to be. I am no longer oblivious and strong; I am dangerously fragile.*

The results of these scans would not only be defining Ari's future, but mine as well.

CHAPTER 22

UNDYING (THE NEXT DAY)

Dr. Tallon's form was blurry from across the table in the conference room and her movements seemed exaggerated and slightly unpredictable.

In an effort to chase away the lightheaded-dizzy feeling, I blinked a few times. It didn't seem to help. *At least I can hear properly. I just need to hear the results of Ari's MIBG scan. They need to be good.*

I focused hard on the silhouette in front of me. Everything felt distant. I blinked hard once again. It didn't help. But if something was wrong with me, I would deal with it after I heard the results.

"I have fantastic news," Dr. Tallon began. "Ari's latest MIBG scan shows no cancer. Nothing lit up. It's a miracle. Ari has gone into—what the oncology field calls—spontaneous remission."

My heart beat with undying optimism.

"Wait, really? Oh my gosh! That's amazing? So she doesn't need surgery?"

I stared intently at the blurry form in front of me, waiting for a reply. The pause seemed abnormally long, but she finally spoke.

"Well, I think what would be best is—"

"Norah," Ivaan interrupted. "Norah."

"What is it?" I asked, both annoyed and confused. "I'm trying to hear what Dr. Tallon has to say."

Still, he persisted. "Norah, Norah," he said, leaning over to tap my shoulder.

My eyes flickered open.

Ivaan stood over me with his phone in his hand.

"Hey, honey, sorry to wake you. But it's Dr. Tallon. She has the results of Ari's MIBG scan."

I sat up with difficulty. My eight-month pregnant belly felt uncomfortably heavy on my bladder.

Ivaan gently grabbed my arm and helped me into an upright position as I swung my legs over the side of the bed.

"Thanks, honey," I said.

"Of course. Are you ready?" He asked.

"Yeah, I think so."

"Ok," he said, nodding and clearing his voice. "Ok...Dr. Tallon? Are you there? We are both here now."

He clicked a button and Dr. Tallon's voice sounded through the phone.

"Yes, I'm here. Hello, Norah. I suppose we should get started then."

She paused, and some staticky noise came through the phone. I had a guess that she was shuffling some papers around; for her, it seemed habitual before beginning a conversation. I imagined her frail, veiny hands shuffling Ari's latest scan print-outs around like a poker player shuffling a stack of cards. *I could only pray she had a good hand. It was an intense game. We were gambling more than money, we were gambling life—Ari's life.*

"As you know, Ari's scans have only shown slight improvements throughout the course of her treatment thus far. Neuroblastoma can be stubborn, especially at Ari's stage and risk type. I was starting to fear that surgery would not even be possible with the minimal progress that we were seeing. However, Ari's latest scans show significant improvement. Only the origin tumor lit up on the scan, and it's much smaller—about the size of a kiwi. Scientifically, I really don't know how to explain this. Ari's curie score just one month ago was 22 and now it's 2. A decrease so significant in such little time is practically unheard of in modern medicine. All I can say is that it must be some kind of miracle."

Ivaan and I looked at each other wide-eyed as we took in this news. *Was what we just heard real?* I considered pinching myself, but my pregnant body already ached enough, so I knew what I had heard was true this time.

"Oh my gosh!" I exclaimed softly, in almost a whisper.

"Oh my gosh!" Ivaan whispered back, smiling. "Oh my gosh!" He exclaimed a bit louder.

All of a sudden, the man in front of me looked younger. The creases and dark circles beneath his eyes seemed to have disappeared, and his energy felt joyfully young. His intense, vibrant green eyes scanned my face. *I wonder if he's thinking the same about me?*

Ivaan looked down at his phone, and realizing Ari's oncologist was still on the other end, he chuckled and cleared his throat.

"Uh, sorry for the lack of response Dr. Tallon. This is just such incredible news! We're both quite stunned at the moment."

"That is quite alright. You should be overjoyed. However, I want to make it clear that—while this is wonderfully unexpected news—we must still proceed with the current treatment plan in order for Ari to reach remission. That being said, there is still a long road ahead, but I want you to hear me when I say this: for the first time, I have hope that Ari can survive this."

Coming from Dr. Tallon, these words meant a lot. Her tone was always plain and direct, and she never gave us hope when there was none to be had.

These words meant that—for the first time—we were allowed to hope.

SLICING DEATH (THE NEXT DAY)

Even though I was sitting in a "comfy" chair in the surgery waiting room, I felt far from comfortable. My leg bounced nervously up and down, and I gripped the hospital's pager tightly in my hand. Lost in my thoughts, my eyes stared straight ahead into nothingness. Still, I could sense Ivaan pacing back and forth to the left of me. Our nerves seemed to be feeding off of each other.

Nervous was an understatement. Even terrified didn't quite define how I was feeling. I was absolutely petrified.

It had been over an hour since we had last received a message from Ari's medical team. At that point, they had removed the bulk of the tumor on her adrenal gland and were about to perform the adrenalectomy. They had said it would be another hour before they were finished. But that was an hour and 17 minutes ago.

A tornado of irrational thoughts plagued my mind. It had existed since Ari's diagnosis, but in moments such as this, the tornado spun with unceasing determination to drive me mad. My filled-to-the-brim with hormones, highly emotional state was not making matters any better either.

I didn't—couldn't—understand the concept of grief in its entirety until cancer metastasized its way into my life. Death causes grief. I knew that much. But now I know that the suffocating, gut-wrenching kind of grief that comes with death can even occur in the absence of death. It's called anticipatory grief.

I wish more than anything that life could go back to the way it used to be—when my biggest worry was if Em or Ari fell down or got sick or felt sad. My imagination of what could go wrong was much more friendly with those worries. Now my imagination and dreams paint vivid pictures of death and dying.

Sometimes I find myself thinking about Ari's last breath. Would I be next to her? Or would I be in a different room? Would I expect it? Or would it be sudden? *I hope I will never have to answer these questions.*

And sometimes my thoughts get even darker. I think about Ari's funeral. The somber flowers surrounding her small casket. Picture boards covered with nearly four year's worth of pictures. Her small, 27-pound frame laying stiffly in the casket and clothed in her pastel yellow sundress. Endless tears falling from her loved ones' faces. The unnatural heaviness of the casket as we carry it to the hearse that would travel to a cremation facility. The unbearable pain I would feel when I hug her one last time; her skin would be cold, her muscles stiff. Nothing of my baby girl would remain except for a small urn of her ashes on the mantle in our family room.

I've only told God about these thoughts—only He won't judge me for thinking so morbidly. The worst thing, though, is that these thoughts aren't even irrational; they're natural for someone in this sort of situation. They're the mental images of a very possible, very dreadful reality.

A tear rolled down my cheek slowly with a bothersome tickle.

Suddenly, my hands started to vibrate furiously. Alarmed, I sat up straight-backed and grasped the armrests of the chair, ready to defend myself. I heard a thump on the floor, and I looked down. The pager was setting off a long, monotonous buzz. I breathed out with relief.

Ivaan came over to me, looking worried.

"Nor, are you ok? Is something wrong?"

He looked at my stomach and then at my face.

I could feel my cheeks flush with embarrassment.

"No, everything's fine. The pager went off. It just startled me is all."

"Oh, so that means Ari is out of surgery right?"

"Yes. A doctor should be out to get us soon," I said.

I looked anxiously towards the doors that the surgeon would come through.

* * *

Ivaan was back home with Emilia now. It had been four hours since Arielle had been moved into an intensive care unit room on Triple C. She had woken up for about 20 minutes once she was placed in this room. Ever since, though, she has been sleeping, and I have been observing. I will never take the ability to watch her chest or shoulders rise and fall for granted. Ari was positioned on her right side with her unicorn stuffed animal embraced loosely in her arms. The back of her gown was unsnapped all the way down to her lower back, and a large, white, square bandage covered the incision on the leftmost middle of her back.

All I wanted to do was wrap my arms around her and hold her tight. But I couldn't. She had to heal. So against my motherly intuition, I watched from a distance—praying desperately that God was comforting my sick baby for me.

The light streaming in from the sliding door to Ari's room momentarily became blocked as I watched a family walk by. A glimpse of their monotonous hospital life unfolded in front of me: the mom carried her young, bald-headed son in her arms, his puffy arm—clearly bloated from steroids—dangled over her shoulder, and the dad pushed the IV pole alongside them. Their faces lacked any expression, although perhaps there was a subtle hint of hopelessness in the father's eyes. They trudged along like army men. No questions asked; they just had to keep moving, keep fighting.

With each family that passed by Arielle's door, I became transfixed for just a moment. I could resonate so deeply with all of them, yet I had no idea what specific nightmare each of them were living through minute by minute. *Did they have a good prognosis? Is it their first time going through treatment? Did they even know what life was like outside of childhood cancer or was this their life since day one? How has the diagnosis affected their family, relationships, work?*

I didn't know the answers to any of these questions, but I could probably guess the general response. If they were here, on Triple C, life surely wasn't all cupcakes and rainbows at the moment, though the staff tried their best to at least make the sun poke through the clouds.

Suddenly, there was a light knock on the door, and as gentle as it was, I'm still startled. A short, petite nurse walked in, her footsteps almost inaudible. She had only been Ari's nurse for about an hour now, but I liked her; she was sweet.

The nurse who started on Ari's case this time around was far from pediatric-material. Maybe she was having a bad day, but it sucks when they carry that to the workplace—a place where so many other people are having *really* bad days. It's hard to appreciate the work of nurses when their work comes off as impersonal, hastened, and merely a task in a series of tasks. Sure, in a hospital as sophisticated as Cardinal Children's, this situation is merely an unwarranted occasion, but when it happens, it's not easy to forget—especially in the midst of emotionally trying circumstances to begin with.

Nurse Myra smiled at me with kindness deeper than empathy.

"How are we doing in here?" she asked softly as she walked towards Ari's bedside.

At first I only nodded, a knob forming in my throat. Then, I breathed in and out deeply.

"We're ok," I said without conviction.

She nodded, her kind eyes fulfilling any sort of response.

Her hand floated up to the heart monitor screen, and she pressed a button, which initiated a low buzzing sound. The blood pressure cuff began to crinkle, tightening around Ari's thin arm. She stirred slightly from the pressure but remained in a healing state of sleep.

Nurse Myra lightly touched Ari's chest with her stethoscope, listening carefully to the sounds of her lungs and heart. Satisfied with what she heard, she pulled the stethoscope away from Ari's chest and draped it over her shoulders like a scarf.

She then pushed some buttons on the IV pumps that were controlling the seven drip medications that were filtering into Ari's bloodstream. Her fingers moved across the buttons like an avid video game players do across a gamepad.

She walked over to the other side of Ari's bed to inspect the surgical site on her backside. Without peeling away the bandage, she made sure there were no signs of infection.

Satisfied with her findings and Ari's state of healing she turned to me once more before heading out.

"Ari is doing well, as well as we hoped," she paused to smile and then continued, "is there anything I can get for you—a coffee, water, snack perhaps?"

I looked down for a moment as if to contemplate my needs and desires. And then out of pure instinct and longing I stretched out my arms towards her like a baby to her mother. Realizing the boldness of my action, I began to draw back my arms. But Nurse Myra didn't seem to flinch; her arms were already wrapping me in a caring embrace, and my shoulders were bouncing up and down through silent wails of grief.

"There, there," she whispered, "I've got you."

And for the first time since being in this isolated room, I didn't feel completely alone.

CHAPTER 24

A WISH FOR LATER (TWO WEEKS LATER)

―――――――――

Streamers of gold and purple stretched down from Ari's bedroom door frame, and plump, pink balloons spilled out from the mouth of the doorway into the hallway. This regurgitation of celebration flowed out into the kitchen, where a pink Bluey cake featuring Bingo sat on the counter, and into the living room, where a couple small gifts waited patiently by Ari's spot on the couch.

The house was quiet for such an occasion. Unusually so—well, at least from what I could remember from this day last year. Ever since cancer became an unwanted part of our family, a certain silence has filled our house. Part of it is the grief and the never ending shock, but, still, a large portion of it is simply the overwhelming exhaustion of it all. When we aren't up and about running to doctor appointments and locked into hospital life, we are housebound—away from germs and catching up on much needed rest.

It was nearing 10:30 in the morning, and everyone was awake except for the birthday girl. Emilia was sitting at the kitchen table, scribbling furiously away on a last minute card for Ari. I watched as she drew a globular body with a skinny neck and legs and a sharp, skinny triangle jutting out of the oval-shaped head. *It's supposed to be a unicorn, I think.*

I smiled and rubbed Em on the back with approval.

"Looking good, love."

She smiled broadly in return.

I walked over to the kitchen counter, and I heard Ivaan's deep voice through the wall. It was muffled, so I couldn't make out any intelligible string of words, but he was talking to *someone* on the phone so enthusiastically that it must be about *something* exciting—*something* worth keeping a secret about.

* * *

A half-eaten piece of Bluey cake sat on a small plate in front of me. I stared at it, and the longer I did, the more blurry it became. I'm not really focused on the cake; it's just a stationary blob for my eyes to rest on while my mind does its regular whirling.

Tomorrow is a day of new beginnings. Ari is set to be admitted later today in preparation for the first part of her tandem stem cell transplant. Hopefully it will be the beginning of a new era free of cancer. So many unknowns and fears flood my mind, but I try to redirect to the present because today we celebrate a day I prayed she—we—wouldn't be robbed of; we celebrate Ari turning four.

Emilia's playful scream broke me out of my anxious whirl of thoughts.

I glanced up to see pink balloons flying up fitfully in the air in response to the punches Ari and Em threw at them.

"Get it Em!" Ari screamed, throwing her hands up to her mouth in apprehension.

Em ran and swooped down in an attempt to smack the pink balloon back towards the ceiling. Though her effort was valiant, the balloon hit the carpet silently.

Em locked eyes with Ari, and Ari frowned in defeat.

Their game of "keepy uppy" had ended, and it was not revivable—only repeatable.

As if on queue, Ivaan came out of his office with his phone held over his left ear.

"Hey girls! Why the long faces? There's an important person who wants to talk to you, Ari!" He held out his phone and put it on speaker.

A young—possibly nerdy—male voice started to speak on the other end.

What is Ivaan up to?

"Hello, Ari! Are you using your best listening ears?" the voice inquired.

"Yes!" Ari giggled.

"Amazing! Alright, I have a surprise for you!"

"Really!?" she exclaimed, her eyes wide.

"Yes! My name is Atlas, and I am from Make A Wish Foundation-North Carolina! Have you ever heard of that before?"

"No," Ari shook her head, confused.

"Well, we grant wishes to kids like you who have to deal with being sick and going to the hospital a lot. We try to make their dreams come true because we know they have to go through a lot of scary things."

He paused as he considered what to say next.

"So Ari, this is a gift from us to you to recognize how strong and brave you are everyday! Are you ready to hear what it is?"

"Yes, I'm ready! Is it a unicorn!?"

Atlas chuckled.

"I'm afraid it isn't a unicorn, but I'll tell you what: it is something just as magical. I heard from your dad that you really love watching the fireflies and stars in the sky. Is that right?"

"Yes!" Ari exclaimed proudly without hesitation.

"Well, next month, once you are feeling strong enough, you will be flying to Norway to see the northern lights! All for free!"

"Oh! Northern lights?" A quizzical excitement painted Ari's sweet face.

"Yes, think of it as the sky coming alive and being really colorful!"

"Ooooo! Like magic!"

"Yes, you are exactly right, Ari! Just like magic!"

"Eeeeeee! I'm so excited!" Ari shouted, hopping up and down and toddling around the perimeter of the carpet.

This is the most energy I have seen Ari express in what feels like forever. I looked up at Ivaan with adoration and a smile. He winked and smiled handsomely.

"That's what I love to hear!" Atlas exclaimed. "Hey listen, you all enjoy the rest of today, and I'll see you next month!"

"Great, thanks so much, Atlas," Ivaan said.
"You've got it! Call me if you need anything."

"Sure thing, see ya," Ivaan said.

Ivaan clicked the hang-up button on his phone and slipped the phone in his pocket.

The girls ran into their rooms like two dogs that have the zoomies.

Excitement coursed through me as well.

I stood up from my chair at the table and waddled over to Ivaan.

"Thanks, baby," I said as I wrapped my arms around him tenderly.

He pressed against me—my baby bump in between us—and kissed me gingerly. His lips tasted sweet like frosting.

"My pleasure, honey."

I smiled and laid my head against his firm chest. He gently rubbed my back.

Yes, I breathed out, *this is the man I fell in love with. He's truly back.*

CHAPTER 25

TWO BECOMES THREE (THE NEXT DAY)

Familiarity isn't always friendly. Hospital life is torture. It never gets any easier to watch Ari go through so much pain and emotions.

But it's *necessary and temporary* torture—at least that's what I keep telling myself.

Ari was in her hospital bed playing a game on her iPad with Em nestled beside her.

Ivaan was working on transforming the couch by the window into a bed for me once again, just how it looked like last night.

I leafed through the *Pediatric Oncology Stem Cell Rescue Transplant - Autologous* booklet that the doctor gave us yesterday when Ari was admitted.

Of course, Ari's team had explained everything optimally, and I've already read through the booklet once or twice, but my anxious brain is always thirsty for knowledge, so I figured it wouldn't hurt to read through it just one more time. Afterall, Ari's stem cell rescue would begin in less than an hour, and I needed something to distract me from my anxious, crampy stomach too.

My eyes skimmed across the words that my ears heard from the doctor just yesterday.

Apheresis- the process of filtering out a certain portion of the patient's blood through a machine and then returning all other portions of the blood back into the patient's body.

Stem cell collection- using apheresis to collect the stem cells that float in the patient's blood.

Cryopreservation- the process of freezing and preserving the collected stem cells for use during a later phase of treatment.

Myeloablative therapy- intensive cancer treatment, usually high-dose chemotherapy or radiation, that destroys the patient's existing bone marrow.

Central venous catheter- an IV that gets inserted through a large vein in the chest, commonly known as a port or port-a-cath.

Infusion- the patient receives an infusion of their stem cells into their bloodstream via their port. These cells will travel to the patient's bone marrow and begin creating new blood cells in an effort to replenish all of their healthy cells that were destroyed by their cancer treatment.

Gosh, my little Ari has endured all of these large, scary terms that most people don't even know how to pronounce.

I looked up at Ari in her bed. *My little warrior.*

* * *

The droning sound of the IV pump filled my ears as Ari received her stem cell infusion. It had been running for nearly half an hour now, so my brave girl was already half-way through.

Ivaan and Emilia were on the makeshift bed by the window playing a round of Go-Fish.

"Draw a card Miss. Fishy," Ivaan playfully instructed Em.

Em giggled and reached up to tuck a thin tuft of hair behind her ear before picking up a card from the deck in between them.

"Your turn Daddy Fish!" Em exclaimed, pointing at Ivaan enthusiastically.

Child-like innocence is a marvel to me. Obliviousness is as foreign to me as overthinking is to Em. Both are dangerous but one is preferable...at least right now.

My gaze flickered over to Ari and my muscles tensed. Her cheeks were flushed and her little teeth were chattering. She stared into space with her eyebrows curled into an expression of discomfort.

Chills. Fever. Of course Ari would experience side effects from the infusion. My sweet girl couldn't catch a break.

After a bit of a struggle against my bloated, tired body, I stood up from my chair and waddled over to Ari's bedside.

"Here honey," I said as I bent to drape a fuzzy blanket around her slight frame.

Suddenly, I felt a gush of wetness seep through my underwear and trickle down my leg. I wrapped my arms around my bulging stomach. *Not now, God. Please, not now. It's too early.* I pleaded with everything in me, but the sensation was too familiar.

My eyes darted over to Ivaan. He happened to look up and his eyes locked with mine. Through panic and a bit of experience, a version of telepathic communication seemed to take place, and Ivaan's eyes went wide.

"Now!?" he mouthed, and I nodded. Within seconds, he was on his feet, and he sprinted into the hallway to find Ari's nurse.

* * *

"You are dilated ten centimeters, Norah. So baby boy should start making his appearance anytime now," the labor and delivery nurse said as she angled her chin above the medical tapestry draped over my bent legs.

Ivaan gripped my hand tightly and smiled.

Though the air was tense, there was an excitement that persisted.

We weren't supposed to be in this moment for another month, but birth doesn't have a good track record for having any consideration for prior obligations. So why would it suddenly work around something so essential such as my daughter's cancer treatment schedule? Right, it wouldn't, so here we were at the hospital—first by obligation, now by chance, and neither by choice.

Arielle and Emilia were being watched by a patient sitter and nurses just two floors below. It grieved my heart to have to leave Ari in the middle of her treatment, but I really had no other choice. Birth, like death, cannot be conveniently paused and resumed on another day.

"Alright, Norah, baby's head is crowning. You have to push now."

I took a deep breath, and I followed through with the doctor's order. I let out a strangled scream of exertion and squeezed Ivaan's gloved hand.

The pain was gnawing. Stabbing. Knife-like. *I don't remember it being this intense.* Tears streamed down my face, and I gasped to breathe through the pain. After another push, my head started to feel fuzzy and my vision went spotty.

Ivaan grabbed my face between his gloved hands, but I barely felt it.

"Nor, stay with me. Please, Nor..." The sound of his voice trailed off even though his lips were still moving.

A nurse began to lower an oxygen mask over my face, and the world around me went black.

Just minutes later, I awoke groggily. The pain was still so intense, but I could breathe a little better at least.

"Norah, honey, I'm glad you're back," the nurse said comfortingly. "You just passed out for a minute from the pain. I know it still hurts, but I'm going to need you to push hard for me a couple more times."

I began to shake my head as I took a strangled breath in.

"I can't...no, I can't," I said so softly I could barely even hear myself.

The nurse's warm eyes rested on mine.

"I know you don't want to do this, honey. But it's the only way you and your baby will be ok. This baby needs to come out now. On the count of three...1...2...3."

I let out an exasperated shout of exertion—crying and gasping for air at the same time.

"Good job, good job. One more time." The nurse encouraged me.

I threw my head back and pushed with everything in me.

As I felt a release of tension, I knew the baby had arrived.

The room went silent. Beads of sweat trickled down my cheek. My eyes glanced back and forth from Ivaan to the doctors.

My heart sank as the nurse whisked a blue-toned baby over to the side-counter.

I tugged at Ivaan's sleeve and looked desperately into his eyes.

"Why isn't he crying?"

Ivaan just stared at me wide-eyed.

I turned to face the doctors and, with my remaining strength, I shouted a little louder.

"Why isn't he crying? Is my baby ok? Please tell me he's ok!" I begged.

I started sobbing hysterically as I watched them do finger chest compressions on my baby boy. His skin was still the hue of a blueberry.

The nurse approached me ever so calmly.

"Norah, your baby boy is cyanotic, which means he's not getting enough oxygen because his heart is not beating properly. We assure you that we are doing everything we can do to help him.

But we are going to have to transfer him to the neonatal intensive care unit for some critical care and close observation right away. We are going to admit you to the women's floor for observation as well."

* * *

As I fidgeted with the corner of the baby blanket that the labor and delivery unit let me take with me up to the women's floor, I heard a knock on my door.

The obgyn, who delivered the baby, entered with a professional attitude. It had been nearly an hour without hearing much, so I was anxious to hear what she had to say.

She gave a warm smile, but it didn't linger very long before it was replaced by seriousness.

"Norah and Ivaan, I want you to know first and foremost that your baby boy..."

"Theo...his name is Theo," Ivaan interrupted.

The doctor nodded and smiled slightly.

"...that Theo is alive and doing well right now."

I let out a breath of relief that I didn't realize I was holding in until then, and I rubbed Ivaan's arm with a smile.

"But we have a few things to discuss," the doctor continued. "When we assessed Theo at birth, he only scored a 1 out of 10 on the Apgar scale, which is a test us doctors use to assess the health of all newborns. As a result, we had to give him supplemental oxygen. His heart was not functioning properly, so we also had to perform an emergency heart surgery to correct the defect. He came through just fine, but he is still depending a lot on oxygen right now. We may have to place a nasal feeding tube in the coming days if he isn't able to take anything by mouth. This should only be a temporary measure to ensure adequate growth and development until he overcomes any feeding difficulties. The last medically significant element you both should know is that Theo has the clinical signs and features of a condition called trisomy

21, which is more commonly known as down syndrome. It occurs when a child is born with three copies of chromosome 21 in their DNA instead of the normal two."

I felt numb to everything at that moment that I wasn't sure I had truly processed anything. *Maybe it's the pain medications?* But Ivaan was just as quiet as me.

"Norah...Ivaan...I know this must be hard to hear right now with everything you are going through, but please know we have resources available to help you navigate this unique path. We want to keep you here overnight for observation. And although we expect Theo to make a full recovery, we want to keep him in the NICU for two weeks or at least until he's breathing better on his own. But you are allowed to see him as soon as you feel up to it."

With this news, the air in the room felt lighter.

Two little fighters in this hospital belonged to me. Despite the shock, trauma, and stress, I couldn't help but smile.

SMELL THE FLOWERS (ONE MONTH LATER)

I cradled my three-and-a-half-week-old son in my right arm as I packed a small bag with my left one. His almond-shaped, beautiful blue eyes and rosey, chubby cheeks made him nearly impossible to ever put down.

Excitement pulsed through me as I imagined the next few hours of the day. Ari would finally get to meet her new baby brother and go outside for the first time after being confined to a sterile hospital room for nearly one month. Her bone marrow transplant had been difficult and left her with gastrointestinal upset and bleeding, which had required her to receive several blood transfusions and forced her to isolate in order to stay away from any germs due to an increased risk of infection. Ivaan called me early this morning and told me that the doctors had said they were planning to discharge Ari tomorrow if all went well, so we could prepare for her Wish Trip to Norway next week.

I smiled again with irrepressible happiness at the thought. We were finally nearing the end of this long journey, and a beautiful light as big and bright as the sun could be seen in the distance.

I heard the soft tread of Emilia's feet as she came running into my and Ivaan's room.

"Mum, can we go see Dad and Ari now?"

"Yes, honey. Just give me five more minutes, ok?"

This was the third time she had asked in ten minutes.

"Fine. Can I bring some bubbles?"

"That's a wonderful idea, honey! Bring your sunglasses, too—and a hat, ok? We're going to be outside the majority of the time."

"Ok, Mum," she agreed as she skipped out of the room.

* * *

Colorful, fragrant flowers surrounded us, and glimmering bubbles bounced up and down in the warm spring breeze. Clouds momentarily drifted in front of the sun, but it was bright out for the most part, so I placed Ari's sunhat over her bald head. Ari was sitting on my lap, and her usual, exhausted recline onto my chest has been replaced by an upright, attentive stance—like that of a meerkat. Her eyes were bright with wonder and her smile didn't fade as she observed her new baby brother.

My heart swelled with gratitude.

My sweet girl had endured the fight of her life for the past ten months, and she had defeated every obstacle and setback with resilience. There were many days that I thought I would lose her. Yet, here she was—outside for the first time in nearly a month, smiling in the sunlight.

I turned my gaze to my sweet boy. He was now nearly a month old. There were days in the beginning that I was terrified would be his last. Yet, here he was—meeting his warrior big sister for the first time.

Ari reached out her arm, intravenous tubing trailing from its site of insertion, and she offered her pointer finger into Theo's small hand. Theo's eyes squinted open slightly as if to assess the situation, and then he grasped his small fingers around Ari's finger.

Ari giggled with glee.

"Look, Muma!" She exclaimed. "He loves me!"

I could tell she was absolutely enamored by Theo. It was adorable, and my mama heart could not help but beat with renewed strength.

"Of course he does, honey! He knows you are his brave big sister!" I said.

"And he's my brave little bother!"

"That's right, sweetie. You're both hospital warriors."

"Yeah, and tubie warriors." she said as she lightly traced her finger across the length of Theo's feeding tube on his cheek.

I nodded in agreement, only half-smiling. My grateful heart suddenly became tainted with grief, and a sort of invisible heaviness resulted inside of my chest.

They've both been through so much hell so young. It's scary. But right now fear could leave. Love and joy and faith could take over during this beautiful moment of life.

Please, just give me the strength to be present and enjoy it while it lasts.

CHAPTER 27

STARS OVER SCARS (ONE WEEK LATER)

As the plane coasted over to the gate, Ari pressed her face against the small airplane window. She had loved her first time flying even though it had frightened her at first. Theo, on the other hand, made it quite clear that flying was not his ideal choice of transportation—the poor baby had to endure nine hours of it all at once. I made sure to profusely apologize to my fellow passengers for the noise, but I really couldn't do much about it.

The important thing was that we had all survived and made it safely to Norway.

Once we were given the "OK" by the cabin crew, we stepped off of the plane.

I smiled and breathed in deeply. We were finally all together. And to make it even sweeter, we were all matching with our periwinkle "Make-A-Wish" shirts on.

This was going to be a beautiful core memory after so many sad ones, I could already tell.

***

The sky grew darker with each passing minute, and stars began to splatter the sky like white paint on a black canvas.

We laid on a blanket on top of a hill near our resort. Theo laid comfortably on Ivaan's chest, sleepily content with the calm up and down rhythm of Ivaan's breathing. Ari was nestled in the crook of my right arm, and Em laid in between Ivaan and I.

All together. It feels so nice. I've missed this.

I hugged my babies a little tighter. The warmth of their bodies travelled to my heart.

Moments like these are so fleeting; it's what makes them so precious, I think. And especially when cancer is integrated, it's just another reason to really enjoy all of life. Every little moment.

And today was just the beginning. We had three whole months of "living" before Ari would be hospitalized again to receive her second stem cell infusion to officially complete her tandem stem cell transplant and signify the end of active cancer treatment. She had come so far and the end was so near. She would finally be able to start living a normal toddler life—aside from regular clinic appointments, of course, to stay on top of the possibility of relapse. But that was a future worry. Right now, we were celebrating her bravery and strength up to this pint, and boy, was there a lot to celebrate!

The sky lit up with brilliant colors. Even the Northern lights were making their appearance as an offer of celebration.

Ari squealed with delight, and her wide eyes revealed her awe as she looked up at the sky.

"Look, Muma, the sky!" she exclaimed, pointing up.

"I see, baby. It's beautiful, isn't it?"

Just like life.

The sky can be dark—lifeless—aside from a few gleaming stars. And at a different time, the same sky can be so beautifully alive and full of wondrous color.

Nature can be so revealing at times.

Life can be tragic, but it can also be so beautiful.

Tragically beautiful.

I looked around in every direction. The lovely sight of the heavenly painted pink and green blended sky above and my handsome husband and three sweet children to my left and right made my heart beat fiercely with life, love, and gratitude.

All together, I think once more. *How lucky am I?*

I smiled, breathed in deeply, and closed my eyes in an attempt to lock up this wonderful moment as a treasured memory inside me forever.

PART 3: FLY AND FADE

Three months later...

CHAPTER 28

CAPTURING HAPPINESS

Flowers and tall grass tickled my ankles. The hem of my dress danced in the warm summer breeze. A three-month-old Theo cooed in my arms and Ari hugged my left leg. Ivaan's arm wrapped low around my waist, and Em held Ivaan's other hand.

So far so good.

The first ten minutes of posing for our annual summer family photos had gone well, but I knew the kids would start to get restless soon.

As the photographer rearranged us, I handed Theo off to Ivaan and scooped Ari up in my arms. I lovingly rubbed her sweet head, smiling at the soft texture of the peach fuzz on her head.

Now that she wasn't enduring intensive chemotherapy each month, her little body had finally started to heal a tiny bit. Her energy and appetite had returned a few weeks ago, and her face held bright eyes and rosy cheeks. My baby was starting to look "alive" again, and it made me so thrilled. Everything was finally looking up. I just prayed that in five days, all of this progress wouldn't be reversed by her second stem cell transplant. Hopefully, it would just lead to life 2.0 and that would be that.

* * *

The campfire burned brightly in the darkness of the evening.

Long, metal sticks jutted in and out of the fire as the girls tried to toast their marshmallows to perfection. There was a steady, patient focus as Ivaan helped them assemble their melty, gooey s'mores.

Aside from the crackling of the fire, only crunching could be heard as the girls nibbled away at their sweet campfire creations.

Theo stirred restlessly in my arms, cracking open his beautiful blue eyes just briefly before drifting back off to sleep.

Setting her half-eaten s'more on the patio table, Ari got up from her chair and ran into the darkness, her bare feet slapping on the cement before she reached the grass.

"Muma! Fireflies!" she yelled in an excited whisper, noticing her sleeping baby brother.

She was already such a sweet big sister.

Small, lime-green bursts of light dotted the blackness. It was mesmerizing.

"I see, honey!" I whispered back. "Stay close, please. Ok Ari?"

"Ok, Muma."

I watched her small shadowy figure run blissfully toward the green lights, pausing every now and then to send them up to Heaven as she liked to do.

Ivaan put out the fire and picked up a sleeping Emilia.

"Thanks, hon. I'll be in soon," I said, stroking Ivaan's arm as I handed him Theo.

"Ok, love," he replied, kissing the air.

As the sliding glass door screeched to a close, I sat back, letting my eyes adjust to the darkness and searching the yard for Ari's figure again.

She was close, near the playset.

I heard her sweet voice whisper sincerely over and over again as orbs of light flitted away.

"Fly high, firefly. Fly high, firefly…"

A SECOND CHANCE (ONE WEEK LATER)

Ari sipped on an apple juice box and watched YouTube on her iPad as her second infusion of stem cells entered her little body.

This could be it. In a month or less, we would hopefully be done with inpatient treatment and onto maintenance chemo pills from the comfort of home. It made my heart so happy. I was so proud of how far my brave girl had come. She was defying all odds. I just loved her.

I walked away from the window and over to Ari's bed, setting my coffee on the bedside table.

"How are you doing, my sweet girl?"

"Good," she responded, barely looking up from her device.

After three months away from all of this, she wasn't thrilled to be back in the hospital. *Who would be?*

"Aww, honey. It's almost over. I know you're tired."

"I miss Theo. And Em. And Daddy."

A sad, pouty frown formed on her face.

"I know, honey. I'm..."

"I want to go home," she interrupted, whining as tears rolled down her sweet face.

These meltdowns of pure exhaustion weren't uncommon these last few inpatient visits. My heart hurt for her.

"Oh, honey," I said as I climbed into bed next to her, "you'll be home soon, don't worry. And daddy and your siblings are going to come and visit today or tomorrow."

I held and hugged the sad little ball of a toddler next to me. Her tears seeped through my shirt to my skin. She sniffled. I stayed strong and composed, and I let her have her moment.

CHAPTER 30

JUST BREATHE (THE NEXT DAY)

I stared out the hospital window. The moon was nearly full, and only a few stars speckled the black sky.

Nighttime hours in the hospital were the most brutal.

It wasn't even the typical hospital noises—beeping machines, alarms, and IV pumps running—and the regular interruptions by the night shift nurses that bugged me the most—though those things were enough to drive anyone crazy.

It was the loneliness that creeped in and settled in the dark box of a hospital room. It created a vulnerable atmosphere that triggered every possible unwanted feeling: grief, guilt, fear, anxiety, hopelessness. During the long hours of the night, it was just my thoughts and me and God. A sleep-deprived, stressed-out woman talking, arguing, pleading, crying to the creator of the universe.

It was always a helpless, hopeless scene for anyone watching. *But lucky for me, no one usually was.*

Tears streamed down my cheeks as I stared out the window.

Only one discernable word repeatedly ran through my mind amongst other discombobulated thoughts.

"Why?...Why?...Why?...Why?"

Shortly after Ari's emotional moment yesterday, her breathing had become quick and shallow. They had given her supplemental oxygen to help get her oxygen saturation back up, and it seemed to help her breathing a little bit. But then she developed a dry cough and started to cough up blood after a while. They did an emergency chest x-ray and determined that she had pneumonia, which can be a complication of the stem cell infusion and high dose chemotherapy—both of which are elements that weaken the immune system and make a patient more susceptible to infection.

Something about all of this just didn't feel right to me, though.

But an instinct without evidence is hardly worth noting in the medical world. So there I was at three in the morning worrying without direct cause.

* * *

"Muma?"

I jolted awake. It was five in the morning. I had managed to fall asleep for a mere 30 minutes. I turned over on my makeshift hospital bed so that I was facing Ari.

"What is it, honey? Are you ok?"

"I have to go to the bathroom."

"Oh, ok. Let me get your nurse, sweetie."

I shifted to a sitting position and slipped on my slippers. I stood up, feeling a bit unsteady on my feet, and then I shuffled over to Ari's bed to press the red call button for the nurse on the TV remote control.

Within a minute, Nurse Carly entered the room and slid open the curtain.

"Hey guys," she whispered, "what's going on?"

"Ari just has to use the restroom."

I watched Nurse Carly's eyes glance up at the flashing heart monitor.

"Ok. I'm not liking how low her oxygen levels still are, so how about I roll over the bedside commode so that she doesn't have to walk very far."

"Sure, thank you."

"No problem. Give me one second."

She returned quickly, turned on a dim light, and situated the commode close to Ari's bed.

"Ok, Ari honey, take your time sitting up and standing. I've got you," she said as she lifted intravenous tubing out of the way so it didn't tangle.

Ari sat up slowly. I could tell she was weak. She swung her thin legs over the side of the bed and sat there for a second before dipping one foot down onto the ground. Nurse Carly held Ari's trunk as Ari moved onto the commode. Silent moments passed as Ari did her business.

"Why did the lights turn off?" Ari asked.

"What do you mean, honey, the lights are on." Nurse Carly replied.

"No. I can't see anything. Everything's black." Ari explained, a bit breathless.

My heart beat rapidly inside of my chest.

"Ari, sweetie? Can you hear me?" Nurse Carly inquired in a serious, yet calm tone.

Ari's head lolled back and her body went limp. I gasped and froze.

"She's passed out. Let me..." Nurse Carly began to say.

Just then Ari's head lifted back upright, and her muscle tone returned.

"I'm ok." she said groggily.

I locked eyes with Nurse Carly. *Motherly panic met well-calculated reassurance.* Her gaze said to me, "*Just breathe, we will deal with what just happened in a minute.*"

"Ok, Ari. Let's get you back into bed."

Taking a crumple of toilet paper, Nurse Carly lifted up Ari's hospital gown. Then, she placed an arm under Ari's lower legs and one behind Ari's neck and picked Ari up to gently place her back onto her hospital bed.

After pulling a blanket over Ari, Nurse Carly walked over to me.

"I'm going to send an emergency message to Ari's doctor to see if we should order any more testing because of the fainting episode and because her oxygen levels are still very low. I just want to make sure we aren't missing anything since her condition doesn't seem to be improving despite the supplemental oxygen and antibiotics."

I nodded slowly, feeling a bit withdrawn.

"Hey," she said, lightly placing a comforting hand on my shoulder, "we are going to figure this out, ok?"

I offered a slight smile to show my appreciation for her act of solace.

"Ok," I said.

* * *

Ari was asleep in her bed, though her chest was rising and falling quite rapidly, so I speculated her comfort was probably minimal. My poor baby's condition was deteriorating.

I watched Ari like a hawk, barely looking at the doctor as she spoke.

"We originally thought Ari had contracted an infectious pneumonia per yesterday's chest x-ray. However, after looking at her CT scan, we found some characteristic signs of a rare, but serious complication of high dose chemotherapy and stem cell transplantation called pulmonary veno-occlusive disease or PVOD. That is what is triggering the non-infectious pneumonia."

She paused, making sure I was following along.

My instinct now has evidence is all I could think.

I looked in her direction just briefly and nodded, unable to speak.

"Although a lung biopsy is the most sure method of making a definitive diagnosis of PVOD, Ari is too unstable to undergo anesthesia at this moment, so between her clinical presentation and diagnostic findings, that is the diagnosis we are making and will attempt to treat. Unfortunately, this disease progresses quickly and is unlikely to resolve with medication, which means Ari is going to be placed on the lung transplant list."

A tear slipped down my cheek, and I wiped it away angrily.

"Why?...Why?...Why?...Why?"

She breathed in deeply.

"Now, I'm going to be quite frank with you, Norah. We are going to try everything we can to save Ari's life, but given Ari's weakened state, there's a chance the transplant list won't accept her. I suggest you call any family that you want here with you and Ari. There's no telling how much time Ari may have left—it could be weeks, but it could also be hours. I'm so sorry."

Despite Ari's doctor's attempts to hold me up, I crumpled to the floor in a fetal position and started to sob uncontrollably.

Weeks? Hours? I didn't understand. We had been so close to life 2.0. So close.

And now my absolutely worst nightmare was coming to life. I felt utterly helpless.

IF ONLY BAND-AIDS COULD HEAL (TWO DAYS LATER)

My head rested on Ivaan's shoulder. He smoothed back my hair, unsticking strands from my tear-stained face.

The past two days had been brutal. Absolutely devastating. It was one thing to find out the news myself, but telling Ivaan and Emilia about Ari's poor prognosis was far more difficult. It made it feel *too real. Too final.*

Ari was hanging in there, but she was suffering, I could tell. Her body was shutting down. Her breathing was rapid. Her input and outputs were low. Her skin was ghostly pale. Her energy was next to nothing, and she was sleeping most of the time.

It was so hard to watch her little body deteriorate so suddenly and quickly. The reality we were living and facing wasn't kind at all. The chances of Ari pulling through at this point were extremely low. She wasn't responding to any of the medications, and her vitals were only getting worse.

All I've ever wanted since Ari's diagnosis was for her to not suffer any longer, but I had never meant this to be the solution, of course. It was so freaking unfair.

How could treatment have such a cruel duality to it? *What is intended to heal sometimes kills.*

Pediatric cancer warriors deserve better. So much better.

* * *

I watched as Emilia peeled off the paper wrapping around yet another Disney Band-Aid and methodically placed it on Ari's chest. It was her desperate measure to heal Ari.

"I wish it were that easy," I said into Ivaan's chest as he hugged me.

"I know," he said, chuckling sadly and softly, "me too."

"I'm not ready, Ivaan. I'm not freaking ready to let her go. I'm supposed to go first, not her. Not my baby girl."

Tears streamed down my face.

"Norah, me neither. I'll never be ready. Not ever."

He sniffled.

Emilia came running over. Sorrow painted her face.

"Mum, I'm trying. But she's not getting better. Nothing's helping."

"I know, honey, it's not fair. But I know Ari feels your love. I know you must be making her happy just by being here for her. Just think about that ok?"

Emilia nodded.

Then her voice became quieter, taking on a despaired tone with a hint of desperation. "Mum...I don't want Ari to die."

She broke down crying.

"Come here, honey."

Em fell into my arms, sobbing.

"I need my sister, Mum. I need her."

I didn't have any words. Neither did Ivaan.

So we all just stood there at the foot of Ari's bed, crying and hugging.

CHAPTER 32

ANYTIME NOW (FIVE DAYS LATER)

I sat in the hospital bed next to Ari.
The doctors had come in early this morning to tell us that Ari likely wouldn't make it through the next night. Her lungs and heart were struggling to work optimally enough to keep her alive. She was hanging on by a thread, and it could snap at any moment.

Ivaan and Em weren't coming back. They had said their goodbyes. They were now at the hospital chapel because Em wanted to pray for Ari. Witnessing her last breath would be too much for Em, and Ivaan wanted the last time he saw her to be when she was alive. But I wanted to be there—to hold her—until she left us.

Ari was awake and had been ever since Ivaan and Emilia left about an hour ago. This was the longest her eyes had stayed open in five days.

My sweet girl looked up at me, oddly alert.

"I love you, Muma."

I smiled, a tear slipping down my cheek. Her first complete sentence in three days.

"Oh, baby, I love you too. So much."

I squeezed her gently.

"I'm sorry, Muma," she whispered.

"For what, honey? You didn't do anything wrong."

"I'm sorry I didn't fight harder."

"Oh, honey. You fought so hard…" I kissed the top of her head. "…so beautifully."

Silence and sniffling filled the room.

"Honey?"

"Yes, Muma?"

"What if the doctors can't save you, and you have to go to Heaven?" My voice became quieter. "Will you be ok with that?"

"Yes, Jesus wants to see me, Muma."

"You're not scared to leave life, honey?"

"No, Muma, there's no cancer in heaven. I'll be healthy, and I'll have hair."

Taken slightly aback by the directness of her responses, I didn't offer a reply.

Silence and sniffling filled the room once more.

"Muma, don't cry," Ari whispered, "don't be scared. Jesus said He'll take care of me, Muma. He said you don't have to worry. I'll be ok. And so will you, ok?"

My hand slowly drifted up to cover my mouth. My heart hurt as it beat in my chest.

Oh, God, just take me. Spare my sweet girl. Please.

A calm voice from within me moved my tongue, and the painful silence between us peacefully faded.

"I know, honey. You will be ok. Eventually, I will be too."

I breathed in deeply, and it took everything within me to not melt into a puddle of tears right there in front of Ari. *Did I really just say that? How could I? I can't let go. I'm not ready. I never will be.*

CHAPTER 33

FLY HIGH, MY FIREFLY

The star projector that a child life specialist gifted to Ari illuminated the hospital ceiling. I laid in Ari's hospital bed with the slight weight of her and her stuffed unicorn curled up on top of me. It was my desperately improvisational way to watch the sky together one last time. It's what Ari wanted; it's what she had asked for.

I stared up at the glowing stars on the ceiling. A tear rolled down my cheek as I mentally relived the nights when Ari was healthy—when we would catch fireflies and watch the beauty of the real sky. *Together, always and forever, I had promised.*

I looked down at the little girl on my chest. *My little girl.* Her breaths were strained and difficult. Her eyes were sunken. Her head was bald. Her lips were so dry they were bleeding. Her bones were protruding from her thin and tiny frame. I hated to memorize her in this condition but cancer had given me no other choice.

I leaned down and gently kissed her neck, taking in her precious scent. *I prayed my nose would remember.*

She slowly opened her beautiful brown eyes and looked up at me. *There she was, my beautiful baby girl. I loved her with everything in me, it hurt.*

She was too weak to speak, but she offered an audibly soft breath out. The heart monitor let out a continuous beep. For a moment, my heart stopped with hers as grief completely overtook me. I lovingly embraced her lifeless body one last time.

"Fly high, my firefly," I whispered as a tear rolled down my cheek and fell onto hers.

EPILOGUE: FLY HIGH FIREFLY (ONE YEAR LATER)

The sky was sparkling with stars, and fireflies periodically lit up all around us. We all walked blindly in the darkness of night. At that moment, catching a firefly was our common pursuit.

It had been one year since Ari gained her angel wings and flew up to heaven.

Twelve months without her.

52 weeks of not being able to hold her.

365 days of not hearing her giggle or seeing her smile.

8,765 hours without her sweet, small voice filling my ears.

525,948 minutes of inescapable, unbearable grief that physically hurt.

31,556,926 seconds of missing her.

As long as I lived, those numbers would only continue to grow, but Ari wouldn't; my sweet little girl would be four forever.

Emilia and Theo ran past me. Theo wore only his cargo shorts. A light pink scar ran down his chest from his open heart surgery just over a year ago. He was thriving now. I couldn't be more proud of him. Emilia held Theo's hand in her right hand and Arielle's stuffed unicorn in her left hand.

*　*　*

I thought back to the family photos we took towards the end of last summer. It was one of Ari's final healthy moments before things declined so quickly. She was so happy to be enjoying summer out of the hospital and was so overjoyed with her new role as a big sister.

Our family photos were scheduled for the end of next week. It would be the second year in a row that our family photos looked different. Last year, Theo was added in, and this year, Ari's absence would be painfully present.

It would be simple to just cancel them in an attempt to avoid a fresh wave of grief and loss, but by now, I knew better. Grief lingers like campfire smoke on clothing. It threatens to remind the present of the past.

So we would still take those photos to defy grief and to honor Ari. She wouldn't physically be there, but her beloved stuffed unicorn would. Em thought that would make Ari smile from Heaven.

I believed it would too.

* * *

We all stood in a circle. My hands were cupped over a glowing bug and so were everyone else's.

"Are we ready everyone?" I called out so everyone could hear.

"Yeah!" family and friends replied.

"Ok, on the count of three…One…Two…Three…"

"Fly high, firefly!" we all shouted.

I watched as the glowing green orbs fluttered up and away from everyone's hands, and then I looked up at a bright star and closed my eyes.

I hope they make it to you, my sweet girl. I know that when you see them, you'll know they're for you. Muma loves you. Always and forever.

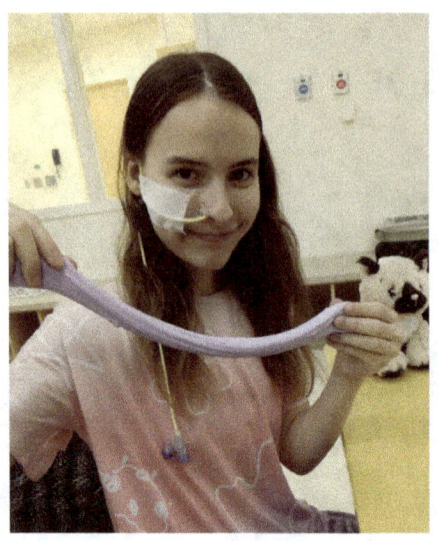

Kyra Faith is a self-published author. Her love of writing began in early elementary school, and she has always dreamed of writing her own book for others to read. She has a passion for nursing and plans to become a pediatric oncology nurse at Mott Children's Hospital. She has a heart for children, especially those facing medical challenges, because she understands the reality of growing up in hospitals and clinics and fighting against incurable illnesses. Her family and her faith in God give her the strength to keep facing her medical battles. She is rarely caught without a smile on her face because she finds joy in the little things in life.

www.ingramcontent.com/pod-product-compliance
Lightning Source LLC
LaVergne TN
LVHW021952060526
838201LV00049B/1674